Karate's Grappling Methods

By

Iain Abernethy

PUBLISHED BY

NETH PUBLISHING

Karate's Grappling Methods

Copyright © Neth Publishing

1st Edition

Published by:
Neth Publishing
P.O. Box 38
Cockermouth
CA13 0GS

Photographs by Peter Skillen
Cover Artwork by IanGordon - ArtStyle - Leeds
Origination and Scanning - Protection Publications - Leeds
Printed and bound in Great Britain by Redwood Books, Wiltshire.
A CIP catalogue for this is book is available from the British Library.

ISBN: 0-9538932-0-0

Please note: The author and the publishers cannot accept any responsibility for any prosecutions or proceedings brought or instituted against any person or body as a result of the use or misuse of the information or any techniques described in this book or any loss, injury or damage caused thereby. Some of the techniques and training methods described in this book require high levels of skill & physical fitness. The techniques and methods contained within this book must only be practised by those in good health whilst under qualified supervision.

Acknowledgements

I wish to express my deep gratitude and thanks to my Sensei, Doug James 6th Dan, for his teaching, guidance and support.

Thanks to Geoff Thompson for his kind words, the much needed advice and encouragement, and for his generosity in providing the foreword for this book. Thanks to Peter Consterdine and Dawn for their help in putting this book together. I am deeply indebted to Robert Gate and Murray Denwood for their help in developing the subject matter, posing for the photographs and for keeping me on my toes. Thanks also to Lawrence McStraw for all his help, especially his part in improving my 'hands'.

I would also wish to express my deep gratitude to Peter Skillen for taking the photographs, his advice and encouragement. Thanks to Tony Mottram for his help and for providing the lighting for the photographs. Thanks to Martin Goodfellow, Ian French, Barry Buglass and Wayne Howe for their support and friendship.

Most of all I would like to thank my future wife Helen and my family for their unerring love and support and for their tolerance of my martial obsession.

CONTENTS

Foreword

by

Geoff Thompson

Renowned martial artist (6th Dan Karate),

self-protection expert and writer.

At long last a credible and marvellous book on the bunkai of karate kata! And not one that just skims the surface looking for frills and thrills, succeeding to entertain but failing abysmally to prepare one for a real, in your face encounter where the winner gets to walk away (sometimes) and the loser gets anything from a plumb eye to a toe tag at the local mortuary. Rather this is an in-depth, thoughtful and thought provoking examination of possibly and probably the deadliest of arts (once fully realised); Karate. Often viewed by the uninitiated as a long range and impractical art for street self-defence, karate has not enjoyed a great rep of late - what with the new wave of realists bringing their cross-training wares to the contemporary table.

To those of us who have really studied - and I do mean 'really' studied - the art of karate, its potency (though often hidden at a glance) has always been patently obvious. When I first studied arts like western boxing, wrestling, judo, Thai etc. and when I first started to teach these arts within my (Shotokan) karate curriculum, I was more than a little surprised (and to be honest disappointed) when my peers accused me of 'abandoning karate' and teaching techniques peripheral to its syllabus. Surprised because the techniques were actually in the karate katas (but not taught on the syllabus) and disappointed because those that threw critique from the bleachers should - if they really did know their system and if they'd actually been in the arena - have known better. I spent a year training as a full time Judo student under the charismatic Neil Adams. What amazed me even more than the dextrously dangerous (and paradoxically gentle) Mr Adams was how much of the Judo syllabus I recognised (much of it for the very first time) from the karate kata. Shime-waza (chokes & strangles), tachi-waza (throws), ashi-waza (foot sweeps), kansetsu-waza (arm locks); all these wonderful and frighteningly potent Judo techniques were in abundance - though often hidden - in the katas of karate. They are a part of karate, but rarely if ever are they taught in training classes up and down the country. And I don't mean the odd kata class where a move is shown and promptly abandoned, I mean dissecting the katas, drilling the moves and allowing them free-reign in the randori or kumite. Imagine now if you were sparring in the dojo and your opponent came in a little too close and you grabbed him by the jacket and applied a cross gi strangle (Heian Yondan) and then threw him to the floor with a wrestler's body slam (Empi kata) and then perhaps followed them to the floor with a little ne-waza (ground fighting). How well do you think that would go down with your Sensei (or your opponent)? You'd be lucky to get away with a severe reprimand. Yet these techniques are as much a part of your karate as gyaku-zuki or shuto-uki. They are as much a part of your martial heritage as the bowing and the OSS-ing. It is not sacrilege that these techniques are unearthed and used, it is a sin that they are not.

I had been thinking about writing a book on bunkai - specifically the grappling aspects as contained in this book - for quite a while but I have been beaten to the post by the wonderful Mr Abernethy (damn his bones!). And I'm glad he beat me too because - though I am loathed to admit it publicly - he has done a better job on the subject than I ever could. The book is very well written, researched and presented, the pictures are clear and unambiguous and it does exactly what is says on the packet. That's why it is a pleasure for me to foreword this excellent text, and recommend the book to anyone - especially those in karate who think they know their art - out there interested in taking their art to the unforgiving, rarely practised grappling range where vertical experts become horizontal neophytes and winning strikers become unconscious grapplers.

Karate possesses a great many close range techniques but they are rarely practised. The main reason, as Mr Abernethy rightly suggests, is that close range techniques will not score points in the competitive environment. I concur completely but I would also add that it is not practised in most traditional clubs because they simply do not know that it exists, either that or they do know but are too frightened to break outside their 'classical' comfort zone. This book will greatly aid in redressing the balance and bring karate back to where it belongs in contemporary martial arts, on the cutting edge instead of dying in the water. This is a great and inspired book.

Geoff Thompson.

Introduction

Karate is most commonly thought of as a kicking and punching system. The scientific principles involved in karate's striking methods make them very powerful. But what are we to do if our opponent gets inside punching range and we begin to grapple, or worse still, end up fighting on the floor? Karate, as it is commonly practised, is at its best when applied at middle to long range. The unfortunate but true fact is that most fights begin close up and almost always include some form of grappling. Are we to assume that a system designed specifically for unarmed civilian self-defence is lacking when it comes to real situations? Of course not, karate possesses a great many close range techniques but they are rarely practised. The main reason for this is that close range techniques will not score points in the competitive environment.

The type of karate sparring that forms the basis of modern day competition was originally designed as a training method to emphasise the importance of quickly disabling an assailant through well-placed strikes to weak points. By fighting in this way the karateka may be able to assure their safety as quickly as possible and hopefully avoid grappling all together. This type of sparring is undoubtedly important, but as time has passed it has evolved into a well-regulated sport. Competitive karate is now specifically a karateka verses karateka affair and the accurate striking of weak points is no longer a requirement due to large scoring areas. That is not to say there is anything wrong with competitive sparring as it requires great skill and many people enjoy it, both as spectators and competitors, but it must be understood that many of its practices run in direct opposition to what is required in a self-defence situation.

At present competitive sparring and its values are over emphasised to the point where few karateka prepare for the very real possibility of strikes failing to stop an opponent and the fight entering close range. Real fights tend to begin at punching range, a few punches are thrown, and if none should stop the fight then it quickly collapses into grappling. The masters of old knew how real fights occurred and this is reflected in the katas they created.

In the book 'Karate-Do Kyohan' Gichin Funakoshi (founder of Shotokan) wrote, "*...in karate, hitting, thrusting, and kicking are not the only methods, throwing techniques and pressure against joints are included.*" A little later he writes, "*all these techniques should be studied referring to basic kata.*" Karate-Do Kyohan also includes photographs and instructions on a number of karate's throwing methods. The Bubishi - an ancient and profound text that is often referred to as 'the bible of karate' - has an entire chapter devoted to grappling and escapes. The Bubishi also contains forty-eight self-defence diagrams; many of these illustrate grappling techniques. The Bubishi's grappling techniques can also be found within the katas. Shigeru Egami in his book 'The Heart of Karate-do' writes, "*There are also throwing techniques in karate... Throwing techniques were practised in my day, and I recommend that you reconsider them.*" The grappling techniques that are found within the karate system are derived from of the Chinese art of Chin-na, the Aiki-Jujitsu of the Minamoto Samurai, the Jigen-ryu Bujitsu of the Satsuma Samurai, the indigenous Okinawan grappling methods of Tegumi, and many other fighting systems imported into Okinawa by the martial artists of the day.

Karate was developed to be an effective and complete method of empty hand combat. It is simply inconceivable that its founders would totally omit grappling - It is the modern day practitioners who are to blame for this omission in many of today's dojos. The founders of our art fully understood the need for grappling skills. They practised grappling, taught grappling and recorded their grappling methods in the katas they created. Even if they are not part of regular practice today, we can see that grappling techniques were part of karate practice and that these techniques are recorded within the katas.

The katas are a vast library of close range fighting techniques and if you study the katas deeply enough it is possible to become a competent grappler. Most karateka simply do not spend enough time studying the katas in the belief that training time is best spent sparring (competition style). Sparring has a vital role to play in the development of the karateka, but it should be based upon the principles contained within the kata. Gichin Funakoshi (Karate-Do Kyohan) wrote, *"Karate, to the very end should be practised with the kata as the principle method and sparring as a supporting method."* The majority of the techniques and methods used in free sparring today have only came into existence within the last few decades. They are sporting methods and must not be confused with the original karate techniques.

The kata are often undervalued, in particular the applications of the kata's movements are rarely practised, and when they are it tends to be in a fashion that bears no resemblance to actual combat. The katas and their applications must be practised so that they can be used in real situations. Gichin Funakoshi in his book 'Karate- Do Kyohan' tells us, *"Once a form has been learned, it must be practised repeatedly until it can be applied in an emergency, for knowledge of just the sequence of a form in karate is useless."* The katas contain a vast variety of techniques that when correctly understood and applied can make the karateka effective at all ranges, including grappling and ground fighting.

Not only will the katas give you the techniques for use at close range but, more importantly, they will also give you the principles behind the techniques. It is vital that you get a good grasp of the principles or you will be a very limited fighter. What if the fight does not unfold in exactly the same way as specified within the kata? If you just understand the specific techniques you will be unable to apply them if anything should alter. If you have a good understanding of the principles involved, you will be able to adapt the technique, in line with the principles behind it, for use in many other situations. This is reflected in Gichin Funakoshi's eighteenth principle of karate-do, *"In spite of actual fighting always being different, the principles of kata never vary."* This application of the kata's principles is behind the statement that it is only necessary to master one kata in order to be able to defend ourselves adequately. The old masters would know very few katas, but they would fully understand the principles that the katas contained. It is this deep understanding that made the founders of karate so formidable.

At first you practice the kata's techniques, from practice of the techniques you can gain an understanding of the principles upon which they rest, you can then practice applying those same principles in different ways and even in sparring & live grappling to further enhance your understanding and skill. You should adapt and experiment with the kata's techniques, not rigidly stick to the exact way they are performed within the kata. When viewed in this way the katas can open the door to a vast range of differing methods. Hironori Otsuka (founder of Wado-ryu) encourages this approach to kata in his book 'Wado-Ryu Karate.' Otsuka tells us, "*It is obvious that these kata must be trained and practised sufficiently, but one must not be 'stuck' in them. One must withdraw from the kata to produce forms with no limits or else it becomes useless. It is important to alter the form of the trained kata without hesitation to produce countless other forms of training.*" In the same book Otsuka also writes, "*Kata must be correct, unlimited and most of all alive. Martial arts progress from kata to kumite, kumite to combat and so on. Kata is a fundamental aspect of martial arts and hence is unyieldingly important.*" This is a profound statement on the importance and nature of kata. Otsuka (like Funakoshi) wished for us to be able to apply the knowledge contained within the katas - just knowing how to perform the katas is not enough. The katas should not be a dead archaic ritual but be alive, unlimited and pragmatic.

The following guidelines are offered to help you approach your katas in this way:

1. Practice and continually improve your performance of the katas.

2. Gain an understanding of the applications. All applications should be practised with real fighting in mind and not as choreographed karateka vs karateka battles.

3. Practice the applications with a partner, who will become less and less co-operative as your skill increases.

4. Look behind the techniques for the principles upon which they rest, e.g. arm bars - forcing the opponent's joint outside its range of motion using your own body in a way that creates maximum leverage.

5. Experiment by applying those same principles in differing situations, e.g. with the opponent in a different position, on the floor, on partners with differing physical builds etc. Be sure to look at how other martial arts apply the same principles and adopt those methods into your training if appropriate.

6. Spar using techniques that follow those principles in order to enhance understanding and skill in application.

Throughout this book I will give examples from the kata and show how they can be applied, adapted and developed in line with the principles the katas contain. Hopefully, this will help you to look at your own katas and extract further techniques and principles. The kata should remain the reference point with all other techniques merely being extracted from them. This will mean that every time the kata is performed, your understanding of its applications and principles will be further advanced and hence so will your fighting skill. I hope to show you just how useful kata can be in preparing you to fight efficiently, regardless of the distance or situation.

CHAPTER 1

Kata & Bunkai

(Forms & Applications)

We have already established that contained within the katas are a wide variety of grappling techniques. Katas are not simply dances to be used to pass gradings or win trophies; they are a collection of very effective techniques (grappling and striking) and as such are worthy of deep study.

The practice of kata brings many mental and physical benefits. These benefits include the strengthening of one's body, the development of fast reflexes and movements, the integration of mind and body etc. However, in this book we are going to look solely at the practical use of kata in combat, specifically the grappling techniques. In many of today's dojos, katas are viewed as being of little use in self-defence situations and as a result are often relegated to the role of physical exercise drills. This is a great shame. In 1908, Yasutsune Itsou (the founder of the Pinan/Heian katas) wrote. *"Karate kata should always be practised with its practical use in your mind."* This chapter aims to show how you can begin to unlock the grappling techniques that the katas contain, and will hopefully also help you to put Itsou's excellent advice into practise.

The first thing to bear in mind is that the katas were closely guarded secrets. In his book 'Karate-do Nyumon',Gichin Funakoshi states that an elderly Okinawan karateka once contacted him as he wished to pass on a kata before he died. Funakoshi was unable to go and asked that the kata be taught to Gigo (Funakoshi's son). Gigo was taught the kata in a locked room with shuttered windows. The old man told Gigo that in his lifetime he had only shown the kata to one other person, and when he did he had crucially altered it. This tale helps to illustrate the level of secrecy that originally surrounded kata and its instruction. A kata would only be taught to students who had proved themselves worthy, and only after it had been practised for many years would the master then reveal the hidden techniques that the kata contained. The katas were put together in a way that was deliberately meant to conceal the techniques within them. This was to prevent the casual observer from learning the methods of a particular master or school and then devising counters or using the skills in a dishonourable fashion. The katas were also practised in secret to further prevent them from becoming common knowledge.

The fact that only a chosen few were party to the katas' secret techniques has led to the creation of a whole new set of applications. These commonly taught applications often bear no resemblance to actual combat. It is important to understand that the techniques within kata are designed for use against violent and untrained attackers, not other karateka. We are very unlikely to face head height kicks or oi-zukis in a real situation and hence it is doubtful that a master would spend much time developing techniques for dealing with such attacks. We have a far greater need for counters to techniques such as tackles, wild swings and head-butts.

If we are to become competent grapplers then we must unlock the secret techniques that the katas contain and begin practising karate as the complete art it was intended to be.

Gaining an understanding of the hidden kata applications is not easy and a lot of time needs to be devoted to it. The best way to begin is to simply ask 'why'? Why am I in horse stance? Why have I just turned ninety degrees? Why are my hands in this position? Try to answer these questions in as many ways as possible and see which solution is the most consistent. For example: Why have I just turned ninety degrees?

1. To avoid an attack?

2. To get my body weight into the technique?

3. The foot movement will unbalance my opponent?

Look closely and deeply at the movement and eventually you will find an application that positively answers all the questions asked.

There are a few key points that you should keep at the forefront of your mind when studying Kata applications.

1. All Kata applications are designed to end the confrontation there and then. Any application that would leave your opponent able to continue the fight is incorrect. Examples of this are the sequences that are often interpreted as multiple blocks with no follow up. You would get badly hurt if you just blocked an opponent's strikes and then turned away in a real fight, so why would you do it in the kata? The 'blocks' themselves must be applied in such a way as to disable the assailant. Remember that kata applications were deliberately concealed, just because a movement is labelled as a block does not mean it was intended to be used as such.

2. All parts of a movement are significant. Hands are not placed on the hips or wound up before 'blocking' as a preparation for the following technique. No movement is without purpose and a good application must take every single part of the movement into consideration. If the hand moves out to the side before coming back in, then both parts of the movement serve a purpose not just the inward part. In particular the application of the hikite (pulling hand) must be considered.

3. Every kata move is designed for use in combat. It is important to understand that all movements within the katas are designed for use in real fights. This includes the opening and closing salutations. Although certain moves may increase strength or improve balance, that is not their primary function. Their primary function is to disable an assailant in combat.

4. The angles at which the techniques are performed are important. You are never turning to face a new opponent. Most fights do not just 'start'; they are normally preceeded by some kind of heated verbal exchange. Statements such as: *"What are you looking at?"* or, *"Give me your money!"* are common examples. Only a fool would not turn to face their assailant before blows were exchanged. The vast majority of kata techniques are designed to deal with an opponent who is in front of you. The main reasons that kata techniques are performed at angles is to instruct the practitioner that they need to be at that angle, in relation to their opponent, in order for the techniques to work, or that by moving in that direction, the transfer of their body weight will aid the technique's execution.

5. The stances are a vital component of the techniques. Stances are never assumed because they look nice, or to strengthen legs, or to improve balance. Stances are taken because they put body weight into the technique or they help to unbalance the opponent. Look at the stance, the weight distribution, the resulting shift in body weight and the manner in which the stance was assumed. Ask what techniques the shift in body weight would aid and you will be one step closer to unlocking the hidden application of the movement.

6. Real fights are sloppy affairs and the way the application is performed will reflect this. Over the years, the way in which the katas are performed has changed. They have been altered to make them more physically demanding and pleasing to the eye. There is nothing wrong with this so long as you remember that when applying the kata's techniques your main concern should be the movement's effectiveness, not retaining an inch perfect performance. What is a graceful movement when performed in the kata will become rough round the edges when applied in an all out situation. Please note - throughout this book the techniques have been demonstrated from a neutral position in order to display them as clearly as possible. When applied from a clinch, against a non-compliant opponent, the techniques will not be as clinical in appearance. The visual appearance of a technique must never be a concern - the only valid measure is whether or not the technique disabled the opponent.

7. The likelihood of the type of attack must considered. The majority of kata techniques deal with likely attacks from an untrained assailant. Karate is a civil tradition and hence its methods were not designed for use on a battlefield against a professional fighter. Kata techniques are more likely to be counters for techniques such as lapel grabs, hook punches and head-butts rather than as defences against advanced combinations etc. It is also worth remembering that most fights occur at close range and hence one would expect the majority of kata techniques to be for use at that distance. Defences against long range attacks, such as lunging punches or long range kicks, may be included but they are far less likely to occur in a real fight and as a result will only account for a very small percentage of kata applications.

8. Strikes should be delivered to anatomical weak points. There should be no doubt that techniques delivered to the body's weak points will have a greater effect than techniques that are not. You should be as specific as possible with regards to the areas struck when studying bunkai. It is not sufficient to say a blow is delivered to the side of the skull, when it is meant to be delivered to the temple, as the resulting effects will be radically different. That said, you should bear in mind that the accurate placement of strikes during an all out fight is nowhere near as simple as some would have us believe.

9. No kata techniques rely upon unpredictable responses from the opponent, however, predictable responses should be acknowledged. It is quite common to see applications that depend upon the opponent performing certain actions; e.g. *"it is at this point the opponent responds with a back-fist."* There is no reason why the opponent should respond in that manner and hence this type of application should be avoided. Some responses are predictable however, and as a result are often taken into consideration by the kata. An opponent who has just been struck in the testicles is very likely to bend forward from the waist and any follow up movements should acknowledge this, and any other similar involuntary actions.

10. There are many effective applications for every movement. If your applications are different from the ones shown in this book, that does not automatically mean there is anything wrong with them. If they work, and are consistent with the traditional principles outlined in this chapter, then they can be looked upon as being correct.

11. Endeavour to understand the principles upon which the techniques rest. The key thing is to understand 'why' techniques work. Try to get beyond the simple memorising of individual techniques and endeavour to fully understand the principles of combat upon which the katas are based. Principles are far more important than techniques. Principles can be applied in an infinite number of ways, but techniques are very specific and hence limited. You should aim to be an adaptable and versatile fighter. Endeavour to fully understand the principles and learn how to fight in accordance with them. Whilst initially this understanding will be on an intellectual level, you should aim to integrate these principles into your subconscious (this being the main purpose of kata practice). At this high level, the body will instinctively act in accordance with these concepts and hence make the karateka extremely formidable. By concentrating on the principles, and the various ways in which they can be applied, the kata becomes an inexhaustible supply of martial knowledge and it is possible to appreciate why the masters of old said it would take more than one lifetime to fully understand a single kata.

12. All applications must be workable in real situations. When looking at applications, ask yourself the following questions: Could this technique be applied when under extreme stress? Is it simple to use or does it require too high a skill level? Will it work against an unco-operative and possibly physically stronger attacker? Is the application truly practical or am I settling for the first application I came across that seemed to fit the kata? Is the technique for use against violent untrained attacks or predetermined karate techniques? All kata applications should be relatively simple to use; they were designed that way. If the application you have come up with is not practical then scrap it and start again.

For every kata movement there are many practical applications, just keep looking.

After you have unlocked a few good applications it becomes a lot easier. You can help this process enormously by asking your instructor, sharing ideas with your fellow students, reading more books on the subject of bunkai and by training on as many courses as possible with senior instructors.

Unlocking the secrets of kata is time consuming and difficult but ultimately very rewarding. Prizing a secret technique from the grip of a kata is a very gratifying experience.

I will emphasise again one very important point - it is much more important to understand the kata's principles rather than amass a collection of techniques. What if the fight does not occur in exactly the same way as specified in the kata? Your attacker may be closer, gripping you with the other hand, physically stronger, taller or shorter etc. If you only understand specific techniques you will only be able to get them to work in specific situations. If, however, you understand the principles involved you will be able to adapt the technique, in line with those principles, to be suitable for use in many other situations. The great Choki Motobu (who was one of Okinawa's most feared fighters) put it very eloquently when he said; *"One must learn how to apply the principles of kata and how to bend with the winds of adversity."* The application of the principles upon which the katas are based are often referred to as 'Oyo' as opposed to 'bunkai' which is most commonly viewed as the direct application of the kata's techniques. For simplicity we shall use the term 'bunkai' to cover all types of kata applications throughout this book.

The Role of Grappling in Self Defence

Although grappling has an important role to play when defending yourself, it is important to understand that grappling is not something you should actively seek out in live situations. It can take time to grapple an opponent into submission, whereas a well placed strike can end a fight in a split second.

Most fights will begin at punching range and it is here that you should try to bring the fight quickly to an end. Before we go on to discuss how this may be achieved, I feel it is important to remind ourselves that avoiding the fight in the first place is by far the most desirable outcome. Gichin Funakoshi (Karate-Do Kyohan) wrote, *"The secret principle of martial arts is not vanquishing the attacker but resolving to avoid an encounter before its occurrence. To become the object of an attack is an indication that there was an opening in one's guard and the important thing is to be on guard at all times."* This is sound advice, when adults fight the outcome can go well beyond black eyes and fat lips, there can be very serious medical and legal consequences. There is nothing to gain and everything to lose by getting needlessly involved in fights. Sun-Tzu in the classic text 'The Art of War' states, *"Achieving victory in every battle is not absolute perfection, neutralising an adversary's forces without battle is absolute perfection."* We must be constantly aware of our surroundings and should an undesirable situation develop we can attempt to avoid it all together. We should park our cars in well lit areas, avoid isolated places, keep valuables out of sight, travel with the car doors locked, avoid suspicious looking people and situations, walk towards oncoming traffic, keep away from aggressive individuals or groups, do not stop to talk to strangers etc. We should be constantly 'switched on'. In this way it may be possible to avoid an attack altogether, and if we can't, then at least the element of surprise is lost to our assailant.

If there is no way to avoid the confrontation then your aim is to 'stun and run'. You should strike the assailant without warning and whilst they are disorientated you should take the opportunity to escape. In a real fight you must never allow your attacker to gain the initiative, there is simply far too much at stake. If you are facing multiple opponents then your initial strike is even more important. It is impossible to fight more than one person at a time, however, if your first strike should disable one of your assailants then your chances of survival will be improved. You should practice your favourite punching range strike, be it a right hook, knife hand, palm heel etc. from a 'no guard' position so that when you are sure an attack is imminent you can unleash that strike, without warning to your opponent, and then make good your escape. It is very important to practice strikes from natural stance with no guard because it is from here that you will need to be able to generate power in real situations. Moving yourself into a 'stance' or raising your hands into a guard will warn the opponent that a strike is imminent and as a result greatly reduce the effect of the blow. It is also vitally important to strike on your assailant's preparation to attack and not wait until you have actually been struck to begin protecting yourself!

It does not take a psychic to see when an attack is about to commence. Your assailant is likely to do a number of the following when their verbal aggression is about to escalate to the physical. Look for a change in skin colour, rapid breathing, an aggressive facial expression or stare, a clenching or shaking of the fists, pointing or pushing, a change in voice tone or pattern, excessive swearing, insults or challenges. All of the previous physical cues are caused by the increase in adrenaline and aggression levels that occur before an attack commences. Be aware that some assailants may appear to be very friendly at first in order to lull you into a false sense of security. When initially approached be prepared for the potential switch from friendly to aggressive behaviour as a means to frighten you and make you more likely to comply with your assailant's requests. Always try to defuse the situation by appearing to remain calm. If your attacker continues to become more aggressive, despite your attempts to pacify them, then continue to keep a sufficient distance to prevent yourself from being easily grabbed or struck (exactly how this may be achieved will be shown in chapter 13). When you are sure that your assailant is going to attack, you should continue to act in a passive manner so that they will drop their mental guard, believing you to be in their control. You should then strike a weak point with as much ferocity as possible. For those of you who feel that this is a somewhat 'underhand' tactic, I will inform you that Gichin Funakoshi and the Bubishi recommend exactly the same approach. Gichin Funakoshi (Karate-Do Kyohan) wrote, "*When there are no avenues of escape or one is caught even before any attempt to escape can be made, then for the first time the use of self-defence techniques should be considered. Even at times like these, do not show any intention of attacking, but first let the attacker become careless. At that time attack him concentrating one's whole strength in one blow to a vital point and in the moment of surprise, escape and seek shelter and help.*" The Bubishi states, "*Often it is essential to deceive an attacker to make an opening. Feign intoxication, weakness or cowardice and when he lets down his guard, strike immediately.*"

Always endeavour to defuse the situation and if that is not possible then try to use the amount of force needed to ensure your safety and no more. You would be legally and morally in the wrong if you continued to strike your opponent after they no longer posed a threat. Having said that, your safety must come first, so be equally sure not to 'under do it'. Always escape the instant it is safe to do so. Your assailant may also have accomplices that you were not previously aware of. Don't give them the opportunity to finish what their friend started.

If you have one well practised technique to use at the onset of an attack, this will remove decision-making whilst under stress and hence help you to respond without unnecessary hesitation. Stun your assailant and then escape, it is in this way that you should try to conduct self-defence situations and not get dragged into long drawn out battles. If our aim is to end fights with one well placed strike that connects without warning, why do we need to concern ourselves with any other techniques? The answer is simple - in case that one technique should fail. If your initial strike should not be successful, or escape is still not an option, then knowledge of close range fighting is a must. In real fights a few punches get thrown and if none are successful the fight quickly collapses into grappling/ground fighting. The back and forth motion of a boxing match or karate tournament is rarely seen in the street. Close range fighting differs from all other ranges in that once the fight gets close in, it is impossible to move back out to a more comfortable range. If your opponent was out punching you, it might be possible for you to back up slightly into kicking range. However, if your opponent is out grappling you, moving back to punching range will be impossible due to the opponent's grip keeping you in close. This is the main reason why skill at close range is an absolute must. You must also be familiar with grappling and ground fighting in practice in order to avoid the panic and exhaustion that close range fighting can impart to those who are unfamiliar with it.

Close range fighting includes both striking and grappling and it is important to use the right method at the right time. When an opponent takes their initial grip, it is not your aim to become involved in a long drawn out wrestling match. The more time you spend entangled with an opponent, the more time their unentangled colleagues will have to repeatedly strike you. In today's society, one on one fights are the exception rather than the rule. Once the initial grip is made, you should use your free limbs to strike the opponent. Remember, when grappling starts, it does not mean it is time to stop striking. As previously mentioned, it can take time to grapple an opponent into submission, but a barrage of focused and well placed strikes can end the fight far quicker. The old masters fully understood this. A great many of the grappling techniques contained within kata, free limbs and position opponents so that decisive strikes can take place. However, if you have no grappling skills you will find it extremely difficult to strike your opponent due to your limbs being tied up. Remember, grappling is to be avoided if at all possible. This is especially true of ground fighting. Your aim when you go to the ground is to regain your feet as quickly as possible; it is not your aim to use all kinds of locks and holds in order to impress any spectators. Ground fighting holds and locks do have their place, but the more time you spend on the floor, the more time your attacker's friends and accomplices will have to kick and punch you.

If going to the floor cannot be avoided try to ensure that your opponent goes down with you. The best way to achieve this is once you feel that you have lost your balance, pull the opponent in towards you and spin so that you land on top. If this is not possible then grab the hair, clothing, anything at all, in order to make sure that you do not land alone. If the worst happens, and your opponent remains upright, turn onto your side and cover your groin with your thigh. Pivot on your hip, using your hands and lower leg to turn, so that your feet are towards the assailant. Use your top leg to kick out at the opponent's shins and groin. If you can gain sufficient space, get up in a way that keeps your head away from your opponent. In all honesty, if you go to the ground alone your chances of getting back up are not good. Whenever you find yourself on the floor, either on your own or with your opponent, you must do everything you can to get to your feet as quickly as possible.

There are a number of significant differences in the way that people grapple for sport and the way people grapple to survive. The majority of grappling competitions do not allow striking. Sport grappling is always one on one whereas real fights tend not to be. In real situations we are not trying to get a win by 'submission' or pin. Originally the locking techniques were used to destroy the function of joints, not to take the joints to their limit in order to get the opponent to tap out. In a real fight your opponent may surrender only to regain their desire to fight the instant the lock or strangle is released; no referee will be there to ensure fair play. Techniques that work well in the Dojo on a willing partner may not work as well on an uncooperative assailant. Perspiration, spilt beer or even blood can make getting the grip required for many locks impossible. Any technique that relies upon your opponent's clothing will also prove difficult if they are wearing flimsy items such as a T-shirt. We must also not forget that many techniques that are outlawed in competition are the norm in a street fight e.g. biting and hair pulling. A major difference is the use of weapons. A technique that will control an unarmed opponent may still allow you to be stabbed by an armed one. The effects of drink, drugs and adrenaline on your opponent's pain threshold must also be taken into consideration. You should keep the information contained within this chapter at the forefront of your mind when studying grappling and close range fighting.

Before we go on to look at the strikes that can be used at close range remember:

1. Stay alert so potential fights can be avoided.

2. If the fight can't be avoided then strike without warning and try to escape whilst the opponent is stunned.

3. If the strike fails, or escape is still not possible, then try to end the fight as quickly and directly as possible using whatever methods are appropriate.

4. Knowledge of grappling is a must in real situations, however...

5. ...Grappling, and especially ground fighting, are things that must be avoided at all costs; they should never be actively sought out.

6. Techniques that work well in a competitive or Dojo environment may not work well outside that environment.

7. At close range, integrate grappling and striking in order to subdue the opponent as quickly as possible.

Close Range Strikes

Karate is full of effective striking methods and I do not wish to dwell on what you are probably already familiar with. The purpose of this chapter is to highlight the methods contained within the karate system that are particularly suitable for use at close range. There are a great many techniques contained within the kata that are not practised anywhere near as much as their effectiveness merits. The main reason for this is that many of these methods are frowned upon in Dojo and competition sparring, for example, leg kicks, head-butts, knees to the groin etc. Obviously this is for the safety of the students, but we should not totally omit these techniques from regular practice, because in real situations there is a vital need for them. Another problem that we have when it comes to close range strikes is that the majority of competition matches tend to stop when the combatants move into close range (this will not happen in real situations). It is here that the referee will restart the bout or the competitors will move back and seek a distance where the more popular techniques like roundhouse kicks and reverse punches can be used. This may lead some students to think that karate is lacking when it comes to close range strikes but it is merely the under use of the abundant techniques contained within the kata that is the problem, and it is an easy problem to rectify.

ONE BLOW - ONE KILL

Karate has been described as the art of killing an opponent with one blow. As responsible martial artists living in today's society, killing your opponent is obviously not desirable! May I suggest that knocking out/stopping the opponent with one blow is a more suitable goal. This does not mean that once a fight has begun we land a single strike and then back off, as is the common practice in competitive sparring, but rather we always try to stop the opponent with every strike used. Miyamoto Musashi in the classic 'Book of the Five Rings' states, *"Contemplate winning all your victories with only one strike."* He also says, *"Go after the enemy with resolute spirit. You must continue to pursue the enemy or he will have a chance to reposition himself, possibly making an even stronger second attack. Do not relinquish your position through any weakness on your part. To do so is deadly and will cost you the battle."* Once a fight has entered close range you must never give the assailant the chance to recompose themselves, and always strive to end the confrontation as quickly as possible. However, this does not mean that you should continue to strike the opponent if you have the opportunity to flee, only that you must ensure the opponent is sufficiently stunned if you are to escape safely. Turning your back on an opponent who is still in possession of all their faculties could be disastrous. The importance of stunning and then running before the situation degenerates into grappling range can not be over emphasised.

In order for a strike to stop an opponent it must have the following qualities:

1. Have body weight behind it.

2. Impact at a reasonable speed.

3. The force generated must be transferred through a strong point on your body...

4. ...Into a weak area of your opponent's body.

5. The blow must not be avoided or blocked (even partially).

6. You must be mentally committed to the blow.

If the above six points are achieved then the blow will have the potential to stop an opponent. Practice your strikes against pads, makiwara and punch bags in order to develop power. There is a big difference between punching thin air and striking a pad, or indeed a person. Make sure you include impact work as part of your regular training. When practising strikes be sure to keep the six points in mind. We shall now go onto look at the striking methods themselves.

Kicks

Kicking does have a role to play whilst fighting at close range, but it is a limited one. Taking a foot off the ground at the same time as your opponent pushes forward can result in you being taken to the floor. Only take a foot off the floor if there is no immediate risk of being unbalanced.

In real fights all kicking techniques should be kept low, ideally lower than the level of the finger tips when the arms are down by the side. Low kicks are harder to block, they do not have as far to travel and the chances of the kicking leg being caught are greatly reduced.

The practice of kicking low is one that is encouraged by the katas. Many of today's karateka kick high during the performance of their kata, presumably for visual effect, however, it is vital to remember that originally all the kicks were low. When using low kicks in sparring, be sure to avoid the knee joint, groin etc. in order to avoid injuring your partner.

Roundhouse kick

An easily applied kick that should be aimed at the inner thigh, outer thigh or groin.

Fig. 1: Low Roundhouse kick

Side kick

This kick is stronger when impact is made with the heel as opposed to the edge of the foot.

Targets include the thighs and the knees.

Fig. 2: Low sidekick

Front kick

Strike using the ball of the foot or the tips of your shoes (if they are strong enough). The shins and the knees are the main targets.

Fig. 3: Low front kick from Pinan Yodan kata

Back Kick

On no account should you turn and present your unguarded back to an opponent in a real situation. Without a turn, the back kick can be useful if your opponent gets behind you. Aim for the knees or shins.

Fig. 4: Low back kick

Stamping Kick

This kick should only be used on a prone opponent if your successful escape or survival depends upon it. Delivering a stamp kick to the opponent's head or chest can cause severe, possibly fatal, injuries.

Stamping the limbs is a safer option that can take the desire to fight out of your attacker. A hard stamp to the legs can also prevent your

Fig. 5: Finish using a stamp kick

opponent from pursuing you. In real situations it is not advisable to attempt to finish a floored opponent with punches. As you drop down to deliver a punch your opponent will have the opportunity to seize either your arm or clothing and take you down to the floor.

If your opponent has secured a grip on you from the rear then stamping to the knees or feet can be a useful part of your escape strategy.

Fig. 6: Stamp kick from Seishan kata

From the clinch you can stamp to the inside of the opponent's knees. This is the application of the 'returning wave kick' from Naihanchi (Tekki) Kata. Choki Motobu (his favorite kata being Naihanchi) once broke an opponent's leg using this technique.

Fig. 7: Stamp to knees from
Naihanchi Kata

Knees

Targets for the knees are the inside and outside of the thigh, groin and (if the opponent is suitably positioned) the face. In real fights the knees should not be used to strike the abdomen. The stomach muscles are in their strongest position when the opponent is bent over and will prevent the blow from having much effect. The knees can also be used to finish a floored opponent by dropping your knee onto their torso.

Fig. 8: Knee strike to the groin from
Pinan Yodan kata

Punches & Hand strikes

The commonly practiced punches need no mention here. The reverse punch, front punch and back fist are not the only hand techniques that karate possesses and, more often than not, it is the open hand strikes that are the most effective. This is particularly true when striking to the head. The bones of the hand are not as dense as those of the skull and if pro-boxers can break their hands (whilst fully strapped up and wearing gloves) then so can you. That is not to say that punching to the head has no part to play, only that very skillful execution is required if damaged hands are to be avoided.

Whilst grappling you must make sure your striking arm has sufficient freedom from your opponent's grip in order to deliver the strike. If your opponent's grip interferes with the arm movement or the shift in body weight then the power of the blow will be significantly reduced. There are a number of ways to free the arm, but the simplest is to violently snatch the arm backwards before the strike is delivered. A lot is also dependent upon where you are striking to, for example, an eye strike does not require as much power as a punch to the chin does in order to be effective.

In the katas you will find a vast variety of close range striking methods. Those strikes should be taken from the kata and practised in a variety of different ways. We will now move onto look at the strikes, both as they are found in the kata and how they are used at close range.

Palm Heel

The palm heel or taisho can be found in a number of katas and does have advantages over the clenched fist. The main advantage being that the palm heel requires less skill to apply and can withstand greater impacts. The main targets for

Fig. 9: Palm heel from Wanshu kata

this strike are the jaw-line, the tip of the chin, the groin and the solar plexus. The nose can also be struck and will cause stunning pain and a profuse watering of the eyes, however, it must be kept in mind that a blow to the nose may not have the incapacitating effect needed to stop a determined attacker.

Fig. 10: Spear-hand from Kushanku kata

Spear-hand

This strike's only suitable target is the throat. Any strike to the throat is extremely dangerous and hence should only be used in life threatening situations.

Knife-hand

The main targets include the carotid sinus, throat and the base of the skull. These strikes can cause great damage and as such must only be used in high-risk situations.

Fig. 11: Application of 'Shuto-uki'

Web of hand

This strike is applied using the area between the index finger and the thumb. The hand can also be closed upon the completion of the strike in order to effect a choke by squeezing the opponent's windpipe. Arching upwards as you strike tends to break the opponent's balance and can be used to set them up for a throw.

Fig. 12: Web of hand from Pinan Yodan kata

Fig. 13: Claw hand from Wankuan kata

Claw- hand

The main target for the claw hand strike is the eyes. The opponent will normally move backwards away from the strike, this backward shift can be used to set them up for a throw. The claw hand can also be hooked behind the opponent's collarbones (if they are prominent enough) to pull them off balance as in the kata application shown to the left.

Fig. 14: Claw hand strike to the eyes

Arching Punches

The hook & uppercut punches are rarely practised in karate circles despite them being found, in a basic form, in a great many of the katas. These punches are very useful at close range as they have the versatility to find their way around guards and stray limbs and are capable of generating great force within tight spaces.

Fig. 15: Hook punch from Neiseishi kata

If you look at the reverse punch found within the katas and then compare it to the one that is commonly used in free fighting, you would note a number of changes *(Figs 17 & 18)*.

Fig. 16: Uppercut from Naihanchi kata

Figs. 17 & 18: Kata & free fighting reverse punches

A. Back hand is now in a guard position

B. Heel is removed from the floor in order to allow the punch to penetrate deeper into the target.

C. The fist is also brought back to the start position on completion of the punch.

If we apply the same adaptations to the hook and uppercut as they are found within the kata, we can now use these 'boxing style' punches to further enhance our striking skill at close range. I will go into a bit more detail here, assuming that you may not be as familiar with this type of punch.

Fig. 19: Start position for arching punches

Hook punch (rear hand)

The punch travels in a semicircle towards the target. The elbow should not open more than ninety degrees and the inside of the fist should be facing you. In order to get body weight behind the punch the hips should twist sharply in the same direction as the blow *(Fig 20)*. Follow through for maximum effect and then bring the fist smartly back to the start position. Stepping across with the lead foot in the same direction of the punch can add extra power.

Fig. 20

Fig. 21

Fig. 22

Hook punch (front hand)

Push your rear hip forwards whilst keeping your eyes on the target. This initial movement will add extra power to the blow but must be performed quickly to avoid telegraphing the punch *(Fig 21)*.

Throw your lead fist towards the target, simultaneously shifting your hips in the same direction as the punch. The arm and fist are held as on the previous technique *(Fig 22)*. Follow through to ensure maximum impact before returning to the start position.

Uppercut (back hand)

Drop the hips down slightly by bending the legs. Push upwards using the legs whilst bringing the rear hip forward. The back of the fist should be towards your opponent. The angle of the elbow should be no greater then ninety degrees *(Fig 23)*. Follow through whilst being sure that the fist travels straight upward and does not come back towards you. Once the punch is spent, smartly return the fist to the start position.

Fig. 23

Fig. 24

Fig. 25

Uppercut (front hand)

This is a difficult punch to master, but the fact that it will often take the opponent totally by surprise can make it a valuable part of your armoury. Push your rear hip forwards as you crouch down *(Fig 24)*. Sharply throw your hip forwards as you push upwards with your legs. As you do this, arc your fist upwards with the back of the fist towards the opponent *(Fig 25)*. Follow through and then return to the start position.

Practice these punches against focus mitts and punch bags to develop accuracy and power. Once competence has been gained with arching punches, you should then practice using them in combinations. Be sure that the combinations you practice 'chain' together effectively. By 'chain' I mean that the preceding punch positions the hips so that maximum force can be imparted into the following punch. A left jab will leave the right hip back and will add power to the following straight right. The straight right will leave the left hip back and will hence set up the effective delivery of a left hook etc. Other examples are: front hand jab - back hand hook - front hand uppercut, front hand jab - back hand upper cut - front hand hook, front hand jab - back hand straight -front hand hook - back hand uppercut - front hand hook etc.

Fig. 26: Head butt from Kururunfa kata - The preceeding movement has broken an attempted full nelson.

Head butt

The head butt is in a few of the katas and the Bubishi gives advise on its use and application. The head butt is an effective technique that is rarely practiced in most martial arts clubs, presumably due to its 'thugish' image. As with all striking methods be sure to use your whole body to generate power. Bend from the waist whilst keeping your chin tucked in. Strike below the eye line being sure to avoid the opponent's teeth. The head butt can be made more effective by pulling your opponent forwards onto the strike.

The butt can also be used to strike upwards and it is also possible to strike with the back of the head if you are grabbed from the rear.

Fig. 27: Head butt with pull forward

Figs. 28 & 29: Upward head butt & Rear head butt

Fig. 30: Vertical elbow from Chinto kata

Elbows

The elbows are strong weapons that can be very effective at close range. Like many techniques they will work well in some situations and not in others. Do not try to force a technique when there is no opportunity for success. Elbows should only be used when close in; you should never try to close the gap in order to use them. Elbows can be applied in a number of directions i.e. upwards, sideways, circular, downwards etc. All of these can be found within the various katas.

Elbows also have a place once the fight has gone to the floor.

Fig. 31: Circular elbow from Bassai kata

Fig. 32: Elbow strike being delivered from the scarf hold

Throws & Take-Downs

As we discussed in previous chapters, throws and take-downs (nagewaza) were always regarded as part of everyday karate practice. It is only in recent times that their practice and use has declined. You will have a large advantage if your opponent has been thrown to the floor whilst you remain standing. Once the fight enters grappling range you must try to take the opponent off their feet as quickly as possible, either by striking or throwing. You should hit your opponent with a barrage of strikes and if the opportunity should present itself for a throw then take it immediately. Do not try to throw your opponent if they are firmly rooted, you must break their balance first. This is a lot easier when they have been distracted by a strike.

A throw on its own may or may not stop your assailant, so once they have been thrown you should instantly follow up or escape. You should not stand back and admire your handy work, as your attacker will be given the chance to regain their feet and continue their assault. You must be prepared for the fact that you may end up falling to the floor with your opponent. Live fights tend to be sloppy affairs and the clean throw does not occur as often as we would like it to.

In practice make sure your partner can land safely and that you are using suitable mats. In a high-risk situation an awkward fall on a hard surface can finish the fight. A Judo instructor once explained to me that, to him, the floor was the biggest fist you could have. Dropping someone onto their heads on a concrete surface can have serious, possibly fatal consequences. You must ensure that your response to the opponent's aggression is not over zealous.

There are many different ways to throw your opponent, with different ways suiting different individuals. Take the shoulder wheel for example, it will not be of much use to someone who is physically weak. Some throws require a higher skill factor than others. In particular the throws that involve turning your back on your opponent should only be attempted in real situations by those with a high enough skill level (unless of course your opponent is already behind you).

Look at the following examples from the katas. You can see that throws rely upon good leverage and an unbalanced opponent to be effective. An opponent who is stable will be impossible to throw, ensure that they are initially unbalanced by pushing, pulling or striking. You should also note that when the opponent is lifted, the lift is achieved through the use of the legs, with the arms being used to guide the fall. In this way it is possible to throw people who are larger than yourself.

Examples from the katas

PINAN SANDAN (Heian Sandan)

Near the end of Pinan Sandan there is the following sequence:

Fig. 1: Basic punch   *Fig. 2: Step Up*   *Fig. 3: Turn, both hands moving with the turn*

This sequence is commonly taught as an elbow and a punch to an opponent to the rear. This explanation fails to take into account a realistic need for the turn and the fact that the 'punching' hand will be around a foot away from the opponent. The sequence is in fact the basic form of a hip throw.

Fig. 4: Seize the opponent's arm

Fig. 5: Step up and turn, moving the arms as in the kata

Fig. 6: Throw the opponent

KUSHANKU (Kanku-Dai) - This technique is often described as two double blocks. A more practical explanation is the one arm shoulder throw.

Fig. 7: 'Double block'

Fig. 8: Step around & complete the movement

Fig. 9: Bring left arm underneath

The first movement shows the initial grip, and the step through teaches how to unbalance and then throw the opponent. Once the opponent has been thrown, their arm is then locked in order to maintain control.

Fig. 10: Grip

Fig. 11: Unbalance the opponent & throw

Fig. 12: Lock the arm

Another good take-down found within this kata is 'the tackle'. The kata gives two options for dealing with an attempted high double grab. You can either go high, or if the opponent is top heavy, you can go low and tackle.

Fig. 13: Arms move to the side

Fig. 14: Fist, open hand & knee all meet

Fig. 15: Drop forward

The application for the first part of the movement is as shown.

Fig. 16: Deflect the attempted grab

Fig. 17: Pull the opponent over by his hair, Shuto strike to the throat and knee to the base of the skull

The next move gives the student an alternative, to go under the attempted grab and take him to the floor.

Fig. 18: Quickly shoot under the attempted grab

Fig. 19: Tackle the opponent to the floor

WANSHU (Enpi)

In Okinawa this kata is sometimes referred to as 'dumping' kata because this sequence results in the opponent being 'dumped' onto the floor.

Fig. 20: Lower block

Fig. 21: Hitch forwards

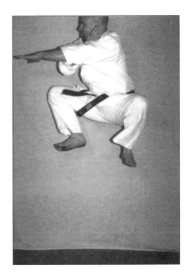

Fig. 22: Turn & Jump

Fig. 23: Land

The grappling application of this move is the shoulder wheel throw and a brutal follow up. It is said that Wanshu - the Chinese martial artist whom the kata is named after - once used his 'dumping method' to throw an opponent down a well! On this, and many other jumps in kata, it is often assumed that the leap is over something or someone. More often than not, the leaps are actually onto a prone opponent and hence indicate the preceding technique was a throw or a take-down. The lower block at the start of this sequence may be applied as a hammer fist strike to the groin. This strike will make the opponent bend at the waist and hence set up the throw.

Fig. 24: Grab the opponent's arm

Fig. 25: Hitch in

Fig. 26: Lift the opponent, moving the body as in the kata (jump preparation)

Fig. 27: Continue the movement to throw the opponent

Fig. 28: Jump onto the opponent to finish

ROHAI (Meikyo)

This is often taught as a sweep avoidance. This explanation fails to take into account the arm movements. Closer examination shows that this is again a throwing technique, and a very dangerous one at that. If done exactly as in the kata the opponent will land on the back of their head. In the following bunkai photographs the arm movement is not fully completed in order to assure my partner's safety.

Fig. 29: Basic punch

Fig. 30: lift the lead leg into crane stance whilst rotating the arms

This throw is done in response to a kick, although is it also possible to apply this throw by scooping the front leg. The Bubishi refers to this technique as 'Tiger pulling down a boar.'

Fig. 31: Avoid the kick whilst moving the arms as in the kata

Fig. 32: Push, lift and sweep to throw the opponent

SEISHAN (Hangetsu)

The majority of karateka explain this movement as a crescent kick to the head with the hand being used to keep the opponent's head in position. Real fights are nothing like the ones seen in kung-fu movies. Trying the aforementioned application in a real fight would get you killed. A more realistic application would be a take-down from a sweep to the knee. The reason the foot travels all the way to head height in the kata is to ingrain good follow through into the subconscious mind of the kata's practitioner.

Fig. 33: Hand opens

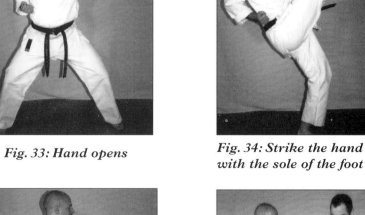

Fig. 34: Strike the hand with the sole of the foot

Fig. 35: Drop back and punch

Fig. 36: Slap the opponent's shoulder

Fig. 37: Kick the opposite knee in an upwards arc

Fig. 38: Punch to finish

These are just a few examples of the many throws and take-downs found within the katas. Although there are a vast amount of throws it can be seen that they all based upon the same principles. These principles, as discussed earlier, are merely good mechanical leverage and the need for an unbalanced opponent. We will now look in more detail at how the techniques and principles found within the katas can be applied

Fig. 39

Technique 1

Take hold of the opponent's arm and pull them towards you *(Fig 39)*. As you do this quickly turn, placing your free arm behind your opponent's back. Feet should be inside your opponent's, your legs are bent and the back of your hips are touching your opponent's legs *(Fig 40)*. Pull your opponent forwards as you push sharply upwards with your hips in order to lift their feet off the ground *(Fig 41)*. Continue to turn your opponent in order to throw them to the floor *(Fig 42)*.

Fig. 40

Fig. 41

Fig. 42

Fig. 43

<u>*Technique 2*</u>

Turn your body sharply, passing your arm under your opponent's arm and, if possible, take hold of their clothing. As on the previous technique the hips should be lower than your opponent's. Feet inside and legs bent *(Fig 43)*. Lift with the hips whilst pulling with the arms so that the opponent's feet leave the ground *(Fig 44)*. Continue to pull with the arms to complete the throw *(Fig 45)*.

Fig. 44

Fig. 45

Technique 3

Grip your opponent's arm and pull whilst the free arm goes through your opponent's legs. As you do this crouch down *(Fig 46)*. Straighten your legs as your opponent's body weight is loaded onto your shoulders *(Fig 47)*. Continue the motion and push with your arms to throw the opponent *(Fig 48)*. As an alternative finish, it is possible to tuck your head in and push the opponent off your shoulders to the front *(Fig 49)*.

Fig. 46

Fig. 47

Fig. 49

Fig. 48

Technique 4

Push your opponent backwards whilst taking your leg to the outside and past their leg (Fig 50). Continue to push your opponent backwards and at the same time pull your own leg sharply back to complete the throw (Fig 51).

Fig. 50

Fig. 51

Technique 5

Take your leg past and behind your opponent's leg, going to the inside *(Fig 52)*. Push sharply forwards whilst pulling your leg back in order to complete the throw *(Fig 53)*.

Fig. 52

Fig. 53

Technique 6

As your opponent kicks, slip to the outside parrying the kick with your forearm *(Fig 54)*. Continue the movement of the parrying arm in order to catch the leg. At the same time place your free hand on your opponent's chest *(Fig 55)*.

Fig. 54

Fig. 55

Fig. 56

Fig. 57

Lift the opponent's leg and push hard on their chest whilst sweeping out their supporting leg with your lead foot *(Fig 56)*. As mentioned earlier it is possible to begin this throw by scooping the leg. Move to the outside, placing one arm behind the leg whilst the other goes to the opponent's chest *(Fig 57)*. Lift the leg and continue the throw as before.

Technique 7

The sweep is a simple but effective technique and is used by practically all karateka. The sole of the foot is used against the opponent's ankle in order to knock them off balance. The hips are the source of power and it is vital to take them fully through if the sweep is going to be effective *(Fig 58)*.

Fig. 58

If the opponent does not immediately fall to the floor, you must take advantage of the opponent's imbalance by impacting strongly with a suitable technique *(Fig 59)*. This impact may well finish the job by knocking the opponent to the floor.

Fig. 59

Technique 8

For the reverse sweep the foot is positioned to the outside of the opponent's lead leg and hooked sharply backwards. If the clothing is seized around the opponent's lead shoulder their upper body can be pushed sharply towards the floor at the same time as the sweep. This push greatly aids taking the opponent to the floor *(Fig 60)*.

Fig. 60

This sweep can also be used when the opponent has failed to retract their kicking leg fast enough. In the dojo the opponent's upper body is held to prevent injury *(Fig 61)*. In a high-risk situation the opponent can be violently pushed to increase the impact.

Fig. 61

Technique 9

The tackle is often used in competitive grappling as a means to take the fight to the floor. As discussed in chapter two, a floor fight is to be avoided at all costs in a real situation. So long as you stand up the instant the opponent has hit the floor, and tackle low enough to prevent them from grabbing you, then the tackle can be used effectively. Personally, I would not use the tackle from the upright position for fear of getting involved in a floor fight, being kneed or kicked in the head as I dropped (by the assailant or any of their accomplices) or getting caught in a front choke. If I were already down however then the tackle would be a good way to even things up.

The opponent has knocked you to your knees. Dive forwards strongly, putting your shoulder into your opponent's knees as your arms wrap around the legs *(Fig 62)*. Push with the legs and keep a tight hold until the opponent hits the floor *(Fig 63)*. Once the opponent is down, quickly regain your feet and prepare to finish.

Fig. 62

Fig. 63

Technique 10

This is a simple but effective take-down that can be found at the end of Pinan Shodan / Heian Nidan and is often labeled as a 'double block'. The Technique is also recorded in the Bubishi and is referred to as, "Little demons remove their boots." You have caught the opponents kicking leg *(Fig 64)*. Step forwards as you lift the leg in order to take the opponent off balance and hence onto the floor *(Fig 65)*.

There are many other throws and take-downs and I would encourage you to look at your katas, the principles they contain, and the throwing methods of other styles in order to further develop your knowledge and skills. The most important thing, however, is to have a handful of techniques that you have drilled repeatedly and are capable of executing in high risk, high stress situations.

We will see a few more take-downs in the other chapters. By locking a joint, an opponent can be forced onto the floor. Because these techniques rely upon a joint lock they are to be included in the relevant chapter.

Fig. 64   Fig. 65

CHAPTER 5

Chokes & Strangles

Chokes and strangles (Shime-waza) are extremely effective when applied correctly. The recipient of a secure choke or strangle will lapse into unconsciousness in around three to five seconds. If the hold is kept on for any length of time after unconsciousness has set in, brain damage or even death may occur. Chokes and strangles are very dangerous techniques that deserve the utmost respect. Great care must be taken in practice in order to avoid injuries; chokes and strangles must always be practised under qualified supervision. When practising with a partner, always release the hold the instant they tap.

Chokes and Strangles are relatively easy to learn and will definitely stop an opponent, regardless of size, if used correctly. They are particularly good for finishing when the fight has gone to the ground. Chokes and strangles can be broadly placed into two categories, those that rely upon the opponent's clothing for leverage and those that do not. The ones that do not rely upon clothing are often referred to as 'naked' chokes or strangles. A flimsy T-shirt will not give the same amount of leverage as a Judo gi. Before employing techniques against clothing be sure that it is strong enough to support the technique's execution.

The difference between a choke and a strangle is that a choke cuts off air, whereas a strangle cuts off blood. Chokes are applied across the windpipe and prevent the recipient from taking air into the lungs. You must exercise caution when practising chokes, as it is very easy to damage the windpipe. Strangles are applied to the carotid sinus and prevent oxygenated blood from reaching the brain.

Once the choke or strangle is applied you must be prepared for the opponent to begin to thrash around wildly in an attempt to escape. So long as the hold remains secure, this thrashing about will only serve to further weaken the opponent by draining their energy.

We will now look at a few examples of chokes and strangles as they are found within the katas.

PINAN NIDAN (Heian Shodan)

The head block is found in many different katas.

Fig. 1: Basic head block   *Fig. 2: Assisted forearm choke*

The basic head 'block' has a number of different applications, one of which is an assisted choke. The pulling hand is used to grip the opponent's wrist and hence limit the opponent's ability to strike or escape. This technique needs something solid to be behind the opponent in order to be applied, this could be a wall, a car or a pillar etc.

PINAN GODAN (Heian Godan)

The following sequence is found at the start of the kata.

Fig. 3: 'Outer block'

Fig. 4: Punch

Fig. 5: Draw up to 'guard'

The application of this sequence starts as your wrist has been grabbed. A joint manipulation technique is used to throw the opponent off balance, followed by a punch to the ribs and then stepping up to choke the now off balance opponent.

Fig. 6: Start positioning

Fig. 7: Move to the side and manipulate the arm

Fig. 8: Punch

Fig. 9: Step in and pull the opponent around before applying the choke

Later in the kata the following position is assumed after a jump.

Fig. 10: Lower cross block

The preceding movement has thrown the opponent to the floor. The jump knocks the wind out of the opponent as the knee hits the ribcage. The rear foot is used to secure the opponent's arm against their body. The body weight is pushed onto the knee to further hamper the breathing as the gi is grabbed to apply a strangle using the forearms.

Fig. 11: Cross strangle

ROHAI (meikyo)

This sequence is found in the version of Rohai practised by Wado-Ryu stylists.

Fig. 12: Horse stance

Fig. 13: 180 degree turn

Fig. 14: Slowly pull both hands to the hips

The kata shows a simultaneous hammerlock and choke.

The opponent's punch is blocked, you move behind the opponent, lock the arm and then pull backwards to apply the choke. If the opponent tries to move away from the lock they will enhance the effect of the choke and vice-versa.

Fig. 15: Block

Fig. 16: move behind and lock

From the examples within the katas you can see many similarities and underlying principles. The opponent's body is always secured either through pushing them against a wall or the floor, through pulling the opponent against your own body or through the application of a lock. The limbs are used in a way that creates good leverage and a secure hold. The air way or blood flow is cut off using pressure from the limbs. The kata also positions either you or your opponent first, so that the application of the technique is possible. We will now move onto look at how the techniques and

Fig. 17: pull in to apply the choke

principles of the chokes & strangles as found within the karate kata can be applied.

Fig. 18

Technique 1 (basic choke)

The forearm is passed across the lower part of the recipient's windpipe and the hands are clasped together. Both arms are pulled backwards using the muscles of the back to apply pressure to the windpipe. The back of the opponent's head and neck are firmly against your chest *(Fig 18)*. Make sure the elbow of the choking arm is also pulled backwards at the same time as the hands to ensure that the forearm remains straight, otherwise the choke will be ineffective.

Technique 2 (basic strangle)

Your arm is passed across your opponent's neck so that your elbow is in line with the centre of the throat. The arm is bent in a 'V' shape so that the hand comes over your opponent's shoulder. Keep your own body tightly up against your opponent's back. Place your free hand onto the hand of the strangling arm. Push so that the forearm and the biceps place pressure onto the carotid sinus on both sides of the neck *(Fig 19)*.

Fig. 19

Technique 3

An effective variation is to place the hand of the strangling arm onto your own upper arm. You can then use your arm to augment the strangle whilst the hand pushes down on the back of the head *(Fig 20)*. As with all chokes and strangles, this technique can also be used whilst floor fighting *(Fig 21)*.

Fig. 20

Fig. 21

Technique 4

This technique requires that the opponent is wearing strong clothing in order to be effective. If your opponent were wearing a shirt or a T-shirt you would be well advised to use another method. You should take as deep a hold as is possible, thumbs going inside the jacket or the neck of the clothing. Push against the arteries of the neck using the forearms in a 'scissor' like motion to complete the strangle *(Fig 22)*.

Fig. 22

This technique can also be used from underneath your opponent *(Fig 23)*.

Fig. 23

Technique 5

Whilst fighting on the floor, seize the opponent's shoulder, placing your forearm across their windpipe. Place your weight onto your forearm to complete the choke *(Fig 24)*.

Fig. 24

Technique 6

Take your arm past your opponent's head *(Fig 25)*. Circle your arm around the opponent's neck so that the forearm is across the throat and clasp your hands together. Close the choke by pulling the forearm upward.

Fig. 25

Fig. 26

As you tighten your grip stand upright in order to apply the greatest possible pressure *(Fig 26)*.

Fig. 27

This choke is useful if your opponent should try to tackle you. Kick your legs backwards so the opponent's arms can not encircle them *(Fig 27)*.

Then apply the choke as before, being sure to straighten up fully once the grip is secure. It is also possible to use this technique from underneath your opponent *(Fig 28)*.

Fig. 28

Technique 7

It is also possible to choke and strangle the opponent using the legs. Leg chokes are far more difficult to apply and should only be used in real situations by those with a high enough skill level. Push your opponent's arm backwards as you raise your knee *(Fig 29)*.

Fig. 29

Fig. 30

Swing your leg onto your opponent's shoulder with your shin being placed across their back. Be sure to retain control of the opponent's free hand. Lift your other leg so that the back of the knee is used to secure the leg across the opponent's back. You may use your free hand to pull the foot into position if necessary *(Fig 30)*.

Push the opponent's free arm under their chin and then pull their head down as far as possible to secure the technique *(Fig 31)*. You can also strike the opponent from this position if necessary.

Fig. 31

CHAPTER 6

Arm Bars

Arm bars have a limited role in live fights. As a result of the high levels of physical exertion and adrenalin experienced during fights, both you and your opponent are likely to sweat heavily. This, and any blood that may have been spilt, can make getting the required grips very difficult. That does not mean arm bars don't have a role to play, it simply means that the other, more practical techniques have priority. If the opportunity presents itself then all well and good, but do not go looking for arm bars in the first instance.

The original purpose of locking techniques was to destroy the function of the joints. They were not designed to be used as a form of pain compliance and are unlikely to work when used as such. It is impossible to restrain a violent attacker on your own. You would need around four or five people to have a good chance of success, and even so, an opponent who is controlled is not necessarily defeated. Once the pain is removed there is a strong chance the opponent will continue their assault. Arm bars only have two functions in live situations - to destroy the joint, or as a way to position the opponent so that decisive strikes can take place. When looking at the examples from the katas, take note of how the leverage against the joint is achieved. Good leverage is vital if the arm bar is going to have any effect, especially against a physically stronger opponent. The arm has a limited number of motions. Every arm bar works by either taking the arm beyond, or against, its natural range of motion.

PINAN NIDAN (Heian shodan)

As discussed in chapter two, all the stances have a practical purpose. This particular application gives one reason why the lead heel is off the floor in short cat stance.

Fig. 1: Short cat stance as found in
Wado-ryu's Pinan Nidan

The preceding movement has taken the opponent to the floor. Breaking the opponent's elbow over your knee completes the technique.

Fig. 2: Arm bar from short cat stance

PINAN YODAN (Heian yodan)

The following sequence is commonly taught as a simultaneous kick and block, followed by an elbow to the opponent's chest. This is not a practical application. It fails to take into account the initial start position and the angle at which the technique is being performed.

Fig. 3: Initial position

Fig. 4: Simultaneous kick and 'block'

Fig. 5: Elbow Strike

The following application is more practical and takes into account all parts of the movement.

Fig. 6: Opponent grabs clothing

Fig. 7: Turn to the correct angle and apply the arm bar

Fig. 8: Pull the hair (or back of clothing) and kick the knee joint

Fig. 9: Control the position of the head and deliver an elbow strike

BASSAI (Bassai- Dai)

This sequence gives a further example of how a lock can be used to unbalance and position an opponent so that they may be struck.

Fig. 10: Position arms

Fig. 11: Block

Fig. 12: Twist and drop the body

Fig. 13: Pull and deliver low side kick

The application of this technique is obvious. The opponent's punch is blocked before locking the arm. The now off balance opponent is pulled forward as a sidekick is delivered to the knee.

Fig. 14: Opponent's punch is blocked

Fig. 15: The arm motion is continued in order to seize the arm

Fig. 16: The arm is locked

Fig. 17: Pull and deliver side kick

All of the preceding techniques have locked the arm whilst it has been straight, the following ones manipulate the arm whilst it is bent.

PINAN SHODAN (Heian Nidan)

The first two moves of the kata are as follows.

Fig. 18: Step to the side whilst executing 'double block'

Fig. 19: Move the top arm down as the other arm is moved inward

This move is most often explained as an arm destruction technique, which is exactly what it is. The commonly taught version is that the left arm blocks a punch, to which there is no response. A second punch is then thrown, which is trapped by the left arm as the right hand strikes to the rear of the elbow joint.

This explanation fails to take into account the purpose of the right hand on the first movement and is very unlikely to work unless you are incredibly strong and your opponent has arms like twigs. The technique will cause severe damage to the arm if applied as shown overleaf.

Fig. 20: Opponent swings in a
punch which is blocked by
the right hand

Fig. 21: The arms are moved
as in the kata causing severe
damage to the elbow and
shoulder

If the motion was continued the opponent could be taken to the floor. This technique is referred to as 'Two dragons playing in the water' in the Bubishi. This technique can be difficult to pull off in a live fight. The kata acknowledges this by following this sequence with a strong pull and punch. Should the technique not be there, the kata instructs us to seize the opponent's arm and pull them off balance whilst delivering a punch to the opponent's jaw.

PINAN SANDAN (Heian Sandan)

The following sequence is found at the start of Pinan Sandan.

Fig. 22: Block

Fig. 23: Step up and perform 'double block'

One more double block is then performed before turning and repeating the sequence. There is then a ninety degree turn whilst performing another outer block as in the initial movement.

The technique is not a series of blocks but a throw that relies upon the arm being manipulated. The technique is done in response to your arm being seized as an attack to the opponent's groin or eyes was attempted.

The first six movements show what responses are appropriate depending upon which hand has been grabbed by your opponent. The first three moves deal with a clinch where your left hand is low and your right hand is high. From here an eye gouge with your right hand, or a groin grab with your left hand, has been attempted and countered through the opponent seizing your wrist.

Movements one and two of Pinan Sandan deal with the failed groin grab, and movement three deals with the failed eye gouge. Moves four to six tell us what to do if the initial clinch was reversed. The seventh move indicates that a ninety-degree turn is required to conclude the technique. The application shown overleaf is for your left wrist being grabbed by your opponent's right hand as the result of a failed groin grab.

As previously mentioned, throughout this book techniques that would begin from a clinch are shown from a neutral position in order to display them as clearly as possible.

Fig. 24: Initial grip

Fig. 25: Perform the first move of
the kata whilst pulling your
opponent's arm towards you

Fig. 26: 2nd movement will
twist the opponent's arm

Fig. 27: Turn 90 degrees to
drop the opponent to the floor

The previous examples from the katas are just a handful of the many different arm locks that are found within karate. The examples show the various types of lock that can be employed whilst grappling. You will see that the following arm manipulation techniques are merely variations upon those themes.

Technique 1

Grip your opponent's wrist and twist so that their elbow joint is upward. Place your other hand or forearm just above your opponent's elbow joint. Pull up on the wrist as you push down upon the elbow. Drop your body weight to complete the lock *(Fig 28)*.

Fig. 28

Technique 2

Your opponent grabs your clothing. Grab their wrist with both hands as you begin to turn away from the possible punch *(Fig 29)*. Push down on their elbow with your elbow to lock the arm *(Fig 30)*. The opponent will now be in a good position for you to strike them.

Fig. 29

Fig. 30

Fig. 31

Technique 3

The opponent had grabbed your clothing whilst fighting on your knees *(Fig 31)*.

Swing your elbow over your opponent's arm so that their elbow joint is pointing upward and is under your armpit *(Fig 32)*.

Fig. 32

Fig. 33

Drop your body down whilst pushing up on their wrist, if this is done violently it is possible to snap the arm *(Fig 33)*. You should now get to your feet as quickly as you can.

Technique 4

You have your opponent in the scarf hold. Lift your knee and bar your opponent's arm over your thigh by pushing down onto the opponent's wrist *(Fig 34)*.

Fig. 34

Fig. 35

Technique 5

Whilst fighting on your back your opponent has grabbed you with one hand *(Fig 35)*. Swing one leg over your opponent's arm and past their face as your other leg remains in contact with the side of the opponent's body.

To facilitate the positioning of the legs, place your free hand inside your opponent's leg and use this to twist you to one side (Fig 36).

Fig. 36

Bring both legs downward to take the opponent off balance *(Fig 37)*.

Interlock your legs, being sure to get your leg under your opponent's chin in order to prevent the opponent from biting you.

Fig. 37

Pull down with the hands whilst pushing up with the hips. Keep your opponent's arm in the thumb up position in order to apply the greatest possible pressure *(Fig 38)*.

Fig. 38

Now that the opponent's arm is disabled, quickly regain your feet. It is also possible to lock the arm in this way from the mount position (see chapter thirteen - sequence ten).

Fig. 39

Technique 6

This method is quite similar to the one used at the start of Pinan Shodan. From the mount, grab your opponent's right wrist with your right hand *(Fig 39)*.

Place your left arm under your opponent's arm and place your left hand on top of your right wrist *(Fig 40)*. Pull the opponent's arm in towards their body. Push your left arm upwards and forwards whilst keeping your opponent's wrist close to the floor *(Fig 41)*.

Fig. 40

This technique can also be applied from the side four quarter hold *(Fig 42)*.

Fig. 41

Fig. 42

Fig. 43

Technique 7

A variation of this technique is found within Seipai kata. Circle the opponent's arm and place your forearm just above the opponent's elbow. Put your hand onto your other forearm as the corresponding hand is placed onto the opponent's shoulder. Push down on your opponent's shoulder, taking your shoulder back as you push the opponent's elbow upwards with your forearm *(Fig 43)*.

This technique can also be used on the floor *(Fig 44)*, from the mount *(Fig 45)* and from the side four quarter hold should your opponent try to straighten their arm whilst attempting technique 6 *(Fig 46)*.

Fig. 44

Fig. 45

Fig. 46

Technique 8

This technique is from Rohai kata and was shown in chapter five. The opponent's arm is bent after a low shovel hook or grab has been checked *(Fig 47)*. Feed your arm past your opponent's body so that the edge of your hand touches their elbow *(Fig 48)*.

Fig. 47

Fig. 48

Fig. 49

Move to the side as your hand cuts into the opponent's elbow, whilst your elbow lifts their wrist *(Fig 49)*.

Fig. 50

From this position you have a few options. You can choke the opponent (as in Rohai kata), pull them back by their hair to compound the lock or, as is shown here, place your fingers into the pressure points between the muscles of the shoulder and chest. Pull sharply backward to cause pain and to injure the joint *(Fig 50)*.

Technique 9

The opponent's arm is checked as your other arm goes behind it *(Fig 51)*. The arm that went behind pulls inwards towards the opponent's elbow as your other arm pushes forward and down making the lock tight *(Fig 52)*. Now that the lock is secure, pull your arms towards you and turn in order to take the opponent to the floor *(Fig 53)*.

Fig. 51

Fig. 52

Fig. 53

Fig. 54

Fig. 55

Technique 10

The wrist has been seized *(Fig 54)*. Grab the opponent's elbow, pulling it towards you as you swing the gripped forearm upwards. Twist your forearm so that you can grip the opponent *(Fig 55)*.

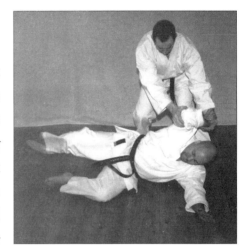

Turn whilst pulling the opponent's wrist down and towards you as the elbow is pushed upwards and away from you, this will drop the opponent onto the floor *(Fig 56)*. If the opponent grips your wrist whilst your arm is upwards, turn your arm to grip the opponent's wrist as you push upward on the opponent's elbow with your other hand. As before, turn ninety degrees whilst continuing the arm movement to throw the opponent to the floor.

Fig. 56

To reiterate what was said at the beginning of this chapter, arm bars are not that useful in a real fight, take them if they are presented but do not go looking for them. Arm bars can be quite difficult to apply. In order to get them to work you must be sure to get plenty of practice.

CHAPTER 7

Leg & Ankle Locks

T here are many different types of leg lock. The majority of leg locks taught throughout the martial arts are used as finishing techniques whilst floor fighting. However, leg locks can also be used whilst vertical as a means to take the opponent to the ground.

Dropping down in an attempt to lock the legs can leave you very vulnerable to being kicked or kneed in the head. If your opponent has already gained an advantage by knocking you to your knees then these techniques can help to even the odds.

The Bubishi gives instruction on a few legs locks and also gives recommendations on their use. The techniques shown in the Bubishi are also found within a number of the katas.

NEISEISHI (Nijushiho)

This technique is found at the start of the kata.

Fig. 1: Forearm block

This can be interpreted as a basic leg bar take-down in response to a kick.

Fig. 2: Basic leg bar

KURURUNFA

A version of this technique can be found in both Kururunfa and Neiseishi.

Fig. 3: Ankle hook & push

The Bubishi refers to this technique as 'Tiger close to the earth.'

Fig. 4: Leg lock take-down

We will now look in more detail at these two basic methods and their variations. The knee can not move to the side, and once straight can not move any further backwards. All leg locks rely upon using leverage to move the knee joint outside its natural range of motion.

Technique 1

Take hold of the opponent's ankle with one hand. Place the opposite forearm just above the opponent's kneecap. Pull against the ankle whilst pushing with the forearm. As you do this, move your body forward in order to lock the leg *(Fig 5)*.

Fig. 5

Continue the movement to take your opponent to the floor and then stand up *(Fig 6)*.

Fig. 6

It is also possible to grip the ankle with both hands and use your shoulder to apply this technique *(Fig 7)*.

Fig. 7

Technique 2

Seize the outside of the opponent's ankle with one hand and place your other hand on the inside of the opponent's knee. Hold the ankle and push violently outwards and slightly back as you move your body weight in the direction of the push *(Fig 8)*. As soon as the opponent is on their way to the floor you should begin to stand up *(Fig 9)*. As a variation you can grip the ankle with both hands and lock the knee using your shoulder *(Fig 10)*.

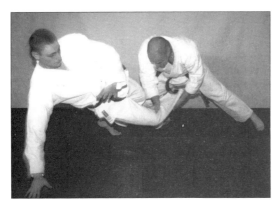

Fig. 8

The Bubishi shows how these techniques can also be applied using the feet. These techniques are for use when you are on the ground and your opponent is still standing. If your opponent is close enough, it is possible to take the opponent to the floor using the leg scissors, but it is very difficult

Fig. 9

to pull off. Remember, your primary strategy should be to kick at the shins and shuffle back in order to buy the space needed to get up safely.

Fig. 10

Technique 3

Hook your foot behind the opponent's ankle and place the foot
of your top leg just below the
opponent's knee *(Fig 11)*. Pull with
your lower leg as you violently push
with your top one in order to lock the
leg and hopefully take the opponent
to the floor *(Fig 12)*.

Fig. 11

Fig. 12

Technique 4

Hook your foot behind the opponent's ankle as you place your
other foot on the inside of the opponent's knee joint *(Fig 13)*.
Pull with your lower leg as you violently push outwards with
your top one in order to take the opponent to the floor
(Fig 14). You can also place your lower leg to the inside of the
opponent's ankle and then kick the outside of the opponent's
knee in order to turn the opponent and knock them to their
knees *(Fig 15)* - overleaf.

Fig. 13

Fig. 14

Fig. 15

Technique 5

If the opponent is on the ground, great damage can be caused to the knee by dropping your weight down onto the joint as the arms pull upwards on the ankle *(Fig 16)*. If the opponent has seized you around the waist from the rear, it is possible to reach through

Fig. 16

your own legs and pull on the opponent's ankle to take them off balance before applying this lock.

Fig. 17

Technique 6

From the side four quarter hold, place your arm under your opponent's knee and lift *(Fig 17)*. Quickly swing your leg over your opponent and place it on the inside of their other leg. As you do this straighten your opponent's leg by placing your

other hand at the back of their ankle joint. Drop back onto your opponent *(Fig 18)*. Fall to the side whilst interlocking your legs and then arch backwards in order to hyper-extend the knee joint *(Fig 19)*.

Fig. 18

Fig. 19

Using the many methods and principles of leverage as outlined in the various katas it is also possible to lock the ankle joint.

Fig. 20

Fig. 21

Technique 7

The opponent has been thrown and you have retained one of their legs. Place your forearm under the opponent's ankle, ensuring that their foot is under your armpit. Clasp your hands together so that the radius side of your forearm is uppermost. Lean back and force your forearm into your opponent's Achilles tendon to lock the joint *(Fig 20)*. In a high-risk situation you could deliver a stamping kick to your opponent's testicles from this position. You can also step across so that the opponent will be turned face down. Pressure will also be exerted onto the opponent's back from this position *(Fig 21)*. Again, in a high-risk situation, you could 'back heel' your opponent's groin to finish.

Technique 8

After a suitable throw, seize your opponent's toes and ankle *(Fig 22)*. Rotate their foot so that the opponent rolls onto their other leg. You should not turn their foot the other way as the opponent may be able to swing their leg up and kick you. Continue to turn until they are face down *(Fig 23)*. The opponent is very vulnerable when in this position.

Fig. 22

Fig. 23

Technique 9

You can also lock the ankle when ground fighting. This technique is most commonly applied when the opponent opens their guard. It is important to wrap both of your legs around your opponent's leg. You must do this in order to keep control and to prevent the opponent from standing up and hence escaping (Fig 24). If your opponent should start to deliver axe kicks, you can kick them in the groin from this position.

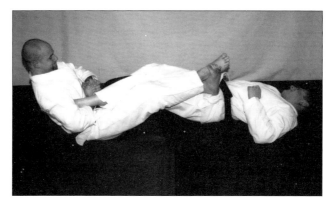

Fig. 24

CHAPTER 8

Neck Wrenches

Neck Wrenches are found in many of the katas. The basic neck wrench is also one of the techniques contained in the Bubishi's forty-eight self-defence diagrams and is referred to as, "An emperor holding the egg." The principle is to twist the neck through two directions at once in order to take the opponent to the floor. If performed violently this method can cause severe, possibly fatal, damage to the neck. Be sure that this technique is only ever applied with force in life or death situations. Neck wrenches must always be practised with great care and should be omitted from live grappling practice.

PINAN NIDAN (Heian Shodan)

This movement is most often interpreted as a turn to block a kick.

Fig. 1: Basic punch

Fig. 2: Step back and turn

Fig. 3: 'Lower block'

This movement makes little sense when interpreted as a turn and lower block. Instead of stepping back, why not just turn on the spot as the kick will then be several feet short of the target? Secondly, it does not make much sense to swing the relatively weak bone of the ulna into the much stronger and heavier leg of the opponent. It is more practical to view the move as a neck wrench and take-down.

Fig. 4: Grip the hair and arm

Fig. 5: Step back and turn

Fig. 6: Take the opponent to the floor

CHINTO (Gankaku)

Chinto - the Chinese sailor and martial artist whom the kata is named after - was said to be an extremely skilled grappler. Because the kata is based solely on Chinto's methods, it is often viewed as being chiefly a grappling form. The following sequence in found near the end of the kata.

Fig. 7: Rising elbow strike

Fig. 8: Hands to hip

*Fig. 9: Move arms and
begin to turn*

*Fig. 10: Completion of
the spin*

If the bunkai were performed exactly as in the kata, the opponent's neck would be broken. In practice, move the neck smoothly and no further than the point of tension.

In the following photographs the movement is not fully completed in order to avoid injuring my partner.

Fig. 11: Pull the opponent onto the elbow strike.

Fig. 12: Seize the hair and place the other hand under the chin.

Fig. 13:Wrench the neck and strike to the inside of the thigh using the knee - In the kata, the spin is then continued which will exert severe pressure upon the opponent's neck.

KUSHANKU (Kanku-Dai)

In real fights, your opponent may try to bite you. The middle of this sequence gives one way in which the head may be controlled in order to protect you from a potential bite.

Fig. 15: Pull inwards

Fig. 14: Spear hand strike

Fig. 17: Hammer fist

Fig. 16: Step around with
back foot

The opponent's head is pulled in so that their teeth are facing away from your body. The head should be firmly controlled between the biceps and the forearm. The turn will place pressure upon the neck and take the opponent to the floor.

Fig. 18: Hand is placed on the side of the head

Fig. 19: Pull in to trap the head

Fig. 20: Turn

Fig. 21: `Opponent is taken to the floor

Neck wrenches appear many times within the various katas but the three examples already shown are typical of the methods used. There are only a few ways to apply a neck wrench and we shall now go onto look at these techniques in more detail.

Technique 1

Place one hand under the chin and seize the hair at the back of the head with the other hand. If the opponent is bald or has short hair, the hand should be curved around the back of the head *(Fig 22)*. Rotate the head diagonally so that the hand on the chin is rising and the hand on the rear of the head is pulling down *(Fig 23)*. Continue to rotate the head whilst moving your body in the same direction in order to take the opponent to the floor *(Fig 24)*.

Fig. 22

Fig. 23

Fig. 24

Technique 2

Take your arm around the back of your opponent's head and seize the hair. At the same time, take hold of the opponent's arm *(Fig 25)*. Take your leg across and turn as you start to move your arm downward. Continue the movement to take the opponent to the floor *(Fig 26)* - overleaf.

Fig. 25

Fig. 26

Technique 3

Grab your opponent's hair at the side of their head. Pull inward so that the opponent's chin is firmly between your forearm and biceps, whilst the back of their head is against your chest *(Fig 27)*.

Fig. 27

Fig. 28

Step through with your back leg and rotate the body to apply pressure to the neck *(Fig 28)*. Continue the motion to take the opponent to the floor *(Fig 29)* - overleaf.

Fig. 29

Fig. 30

Technique 4

It is possible to use the neck wrench to dislodge an opponent who is on top of you. However, because you cannot get any body movement into the technique from this position, an opponent with strong neck muscles will be able to resist. If the technique is not there, quickly move onto some-

thing else. Grip the opponent's head and chin and begin to rotate *(Fig 30)*. Roll in the same direction as the neck wrench as the opponent lifts their body weight in order to alleviate the pressure *(Fig 31)*. When the opponent has rolled far enough you can regain your feet or apply a finishing technique.

Fig. 31

Technique 5

A standing version of this technique is found within Kushanku (Kanku-Dai) kata. Whilst fighting on your knees, pass your arm behind your opponent's neck *(Fig 32)*. Place your hand under your opponent's armpit and begin to pull their arm as you twist in order to take them to the floor *(Fig 33)*. Keep a tight grip on the opponent's arm and lean backward to place pressure upon the opponent's neck *(Fig 34)*.

Fig. 32

Fig. 33

Fig. 34

Fig. 35

Technique 6

From the side four quarter hold, pass your arm under your opponent's neck and back onto their chest. Tighten the grip and roll away from the opponent's head to place pressure upon the neck *(Fig 35)*.

CHAPTER 9

Wrist-Locks

Sweat, blood and a non-compliant opponent can make wrist-locks very difficult to apply. When wrist-locks are practised in the dojo, on a sober and calm practice partner, who will allow the locks to be put on, they can appear extremely effective. The reality of combat is somewhat different however. Knowledge of wrist-locks can be useful but more practical methods must be given priority.

The wrists are very mobile joints and as such can be locked in a number of different ways, all of which can be found in the various katas.

PINAN NIDAN

Near the end of Pinan Nidan (as practiced by Wado-Ryu Stylists) the following sequence is found.

Fig. 1: Basic punch

Fig. 2: Back foot across into short cat stance

This movement can be interpreted as a throw from a wrist-lock. As mentioned in chapter six, short cat stance can be used to apply a lock to the opponent's arm once they are on the floor.

Fig. 3: Grip the hand

Fig. 4: Turn to lock the wrist and throw

PINAN SANDAN (Heian Sandan)

This sequence is repeated three times near the middle of the kata and is often interpreted as a forearm block followed by a hammer fist strike to the chest.

Fig. 5: Fists on hip

Fig. 6: Step into horse stance as the elbow comes forwards

Fig. 7: Hammer fist strike

Standing square, with your hands on your hips, as your opponent prepares to strike is not at all wise. It is also very likely that the opponent would try to punch the head, as opposed to the torso, if the hands were that low and hence a middle level block would not be appropriate. The movement makes more sense when viewed as a wrist manipulation technique. Whilst you are attempting an eye gouge, the opponent reaches up and grabs your wrist in order to move your hand away from their face. You then apply a wrist-lock which will drop the opponent to their knees. The final strike is directed at the kneeling opponent's head.

Fig. 8: Opponent reacts to the eye gouge

Fig. 9: Drop into horse stance and bringing the elbow forwards

Fig. 10: Hammer fist strike

NAIHANCHI (Tekki)

The first position of this kata is sometimes explained as a guard against a groin kick. Obviously this would not work in a self-defence situation.

Fig. 11: 'Salutation'

Fig. 12: Step across

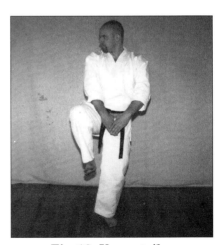

Fig. 13: Knee strike

The opponent has seized your wrist to prevent you from delivering a low attack. You then apply a wrist-lock to drop the opponent onto their knees.

The nature of this lock makes the opponent drop to one side; the step across will then line you back up for the knee strike.

Fig. 14: Opponent seizes the wrist

Fig. 15: Wrist-lock is applied

Fig. 16: Step across and deliver knee strike to chin

Fig. 17: Opening 'salutation'

BASSAI (Bassai-Dai)

The opening 'salutation' of this kata is rarely given any combat application. Most often the opening position of Bassai is given the status of a secret gesture that means that the person performing it has martial skill, or it is given a spiritual connotation. As pointed out in chapter one, every single kata movement is for use in combat.

Fig. 18: Opponent shakes his fist in an attempt to intimidate

Fig. 19: Grip the wrist before moving the hands into the opening position in order to drop the opponent to their knees

The second move of the kata is a diagonal step across and an 'outer block'.

The second movement is telling us that should the opponent be strong enough to resist the first technique, we should move our body weight past the opponent as we perform the lock.

Fig. 20: 'Outer block' after stepping across at an angle

Fig. 21: Step across to take the opponent to the floor

JION

This sequence is found at the start of the kata and is performed at a forty-five degree angle.

Fig. 22: Arms crossed

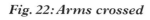

Fig. 23: double 'outer block'

Fig. 24: Front kick

Fig. 25: Punch

There then follows two more punches and then the sequence is repeated on the opposite side. The technique is used against an opponent who has grabbed your clothing. The technique is performed at forty-five degrees because you will need to be at that angle, in relation to your opponent, in order to be out of the range of any rear hand strikes.

Fig. 26: Opponent has seized your clothing. Shift at 45 degrees, grabbing the opponent's hand and elbow.

Fig. 27: Apply the lock, dropping the opponent to their knees

Fig. 28: Front kick to jaw

Fig. 29: Punch the cavity behind the opponent's ear

There are many other wrist locking techniques throughout the katas but the principles upon which they rest are consistent. In order to lock the wrist it must be bent or twisted, or better still, bent and twisted, beyond its natural range of motion. All of those methods can be seen in the examples from the katas and in the more detailed explanations that follow.

Technique 1

Take hold of the opponent's hand so that your thumb is on the back of their hand whilst your fingers are at the crease of their wrist. Rotate your hand so that the opponent's fingers point upward *(Fig 30)*.

Fig. 30

Fig. 31

Place your free hand onto the edge of the opponent's hand. Simultaneously bend and twist the opponent's wrist *(Fig 31)*.

Turn your body in the same direction as the wrist-lock to take the opponent to the floor *(Fig 32)*.

Fig. 32

Technique 2

The opponent shakes their fist at you.
Seize the opponent's wrist as you place
the palm of your hand against the back
of their fist *(Fig 33)*.

Fig. 33

Push downward as you twist the opponent's
wrist in order to drop them to their knees.
(Fig. 34).

Fig. 34

Technique 3

The opponent has taken hold of
your wrist. Quickly place your free
hand on top of your opponent's
hand in order to secure it *(Fig 35)*.
Rotate your hands so that the edge
of your gripped hand cuts into the
opponent's wrist joint and hence
ensures that their arm is bent

Fig. 35

(Fig 36). Seize the opponent's wrist and then sharply bring both hands downward
to complete the lock *(Fig 37)*. In actual application the technique should be
performed quickly, but in practice perform the movement smoothly in order to

avoid damage to your partner's wrist. If the opponent's elbow should become higher than their wrist as shown *(Fig 38)* then the technique will not work. You can rectify this by knocking the opponent's elbow down using your own elbow *(Fig 39)*.

Fig. 36

Fig. 37

Fig. 38

Fig. 39

Technique 4

Take hold of your opponent's hand from above so that your fingers are gripping the little finger side of the opponent's hand and your thumb is between your opponent's thumb and index finger. Place your other hand into the bend of your opponent's elbow *(Fig 40)*.

Fig. 40

Twist and bend the wrist as you move to a forty-five degree angle. Rotate the opponent's hand away from you so that their fingers point upward, simultaneously moving both of your arms downward. This will drop the opponent to their knees *(Fig 41)*.

Fig. 41

Technique 5

Grab the opponent's hand, placing your thumb between your opponent's thumb and index finger. Turn and pull the opponent's hand towards you so that their fingers are pointing upward and the inside edge of their hand is closest to you. At the same time, place the edge of your free hand onto the opponent's wrist joint *(Fig 42)*.

Fig. 42

Cut into the opponent's wrist as you move your hands downward and towards you *(Fig 43)*. The more astute among you will recognise this as the opening salutation from Wanshu (Enpi) kata.

Fig. 43

Technique 6

The opponent has grabbed your wrist. Grab your opponent's wrist with your free hand, ensuring that the opponent's forearm is vertical *(Fig 44)*.

Fig. 44

Keeping a tight grip on your opponent's wrist, step into horse stance whilst bringing your elbow forwards *(Fig 45)*. If done quickly this technique will easily break your opponent's wrist.

Fig. 45

Technique 7

Thc opponent has grabbed your wrist. Secure the opponent's hand with your own hand and then step forward whilst swinging your elbow over your opponent's forearm *(Fig 46)*.

Fig. 46

Move your elbow downwards as you drop your body weight in order to lock the wrist *(Fig 47)*.

Fig. 47

Technique 8

Wrist-locks can be used whilst floor fighting. Here the wrist has been locked in order to augment the application of an arm bar *(Fig 48)*.

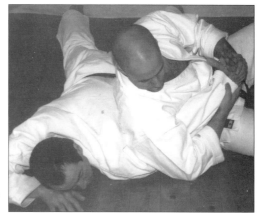

Fig. 48

Finger-Locks

The bones and joints of the fingers can be damaged very easily. Finger locks are painful and can be used to good effect against much larger opponents. The downside is that the fingers can be difficult to secure and even though a broken finger can be very painful, it is unlikely to stop a determined assailant. Although finger locks will not end a fight on their own, they can help to weaken an opponent and are particularly useful as a means to break an opponent's grip. If the opponent has had their fingers damaged they will find it difficult to secure (or re-secure) an effective grip.

The following example from Pinan Nidan (Heian Shodan) shows one way in which finger locks can be used at the start of a fight. However, finger locks are best used during grappling as a means to facilitate other more decisive techniques.

Fig. 1: Pull the front foot back and deliver 'hammer fist'.

Fig. 2: Step forwards and execute a basic punch

PINAN NIDAN
(Heian Shodan)

This sequence is found within the first few moves of the kata. The application for this sequence is a pre-emptive response to an opponent who is becoming increasingly aggressive. The opponent is issuing verbal threats and insults whilst poking their finger towards the chest.

*Fig. 3: Opponent acts in
a hostile fashion*

*Fig. 4: The finger is grabbed
as the body moves backward.
The 'hammer fist' motion
locks the finger*

*Fig. 5: A head punch is delivered
to the off balance opponent*

The kata example shows the finger being bent back beyond its natural range of movement. The fingers have very little backward movement and, with the exception of the thumb, very little lateral movement. It is in these two directions that the majority of finger locks are to be applied. It is possible to twist the finger at the same time as the lock is applied.

This attempt to move the finger in two directions at once increases the pain felt by the opponent. The twist also improves the efficiency of finger locks when they are applied against double joined individuals.

Technique 1

Using the palm of your hand push the opponent's finger backward *(Fig 6)*.

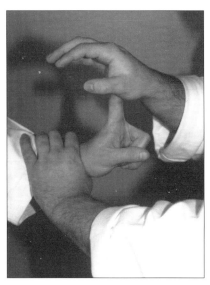

Fig. 6

Fig. 7

Technique 2

Grip two fingers in each hand and pull them apart. The technique is shown here being applied to a prone opponent who has just had their elbow damaged by an arm bar *(Fig 7)*. You should not use this technique against an opponent who is in a position where they could strike you with their free hand.

Technique 3

Grip the opponent's bent thumb with your hand and then crush in order to cause pain *(Fig 8)*.

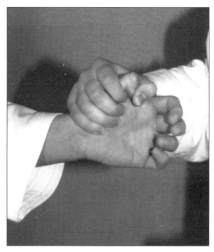

Fig. 8

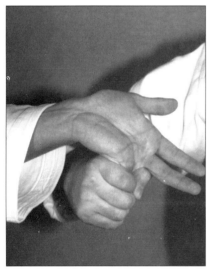

Fig. 9

Technique 4

Grip the opponent's last two fingers with your hand. Twist the fingers so that the opponent's hand is palm up and then bend the fingers towards the opponent's forearm *(Fig 9)*.

This technique can be used to remove the opponent's hand from your throat, or from over your mouth or face. Slide your fingers under your opponent's hand so that the thumb is on the back of the knuckles. Bend the fingers backward to remove the hand *(Fig 10)*.

Fig. 10

Technique 5

Grip the opponent's finger so that their hand is palm down. Flex your wrist so that the little finger side of your fist moves down and towards you.

Move your arm downward in order to complete the finger lock *(Fig 11)*.

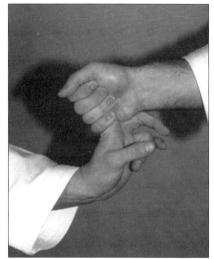

Fig. 11

Ground Fighting Skills - Ne-waza

Throughout this book I have shown how the techniques and principles that the katas contain for vertical grappling can also be applied when fighting on the floor. In order to apply those methods you will have to get yourself suitably positioned and gain control over the opponent. This is where knowledge of holds and pins is vital.

The holds included in this chapter are not designed to immobilise an assailant, but rather to help you to get into a position where you have the advantage. No ground fighting holds appear within the katas, but knowledge of them is important if you wish to be able to apply the kata's methods whilst on the floor. Studying the control methods of dedicated grappling arts will greatly enhance your ability to apply kata techniques on the floor and should be considered.

In a real situation if the opportunity to safely regain your feet presents itself you must take it without hesitation. Do not spend so much time and effort looking for a hold that you miss the chance to get back up. In real situations ground fighting must be avoided at all costs. If you possess exceptional skill on the ground, the fight is one on one and is sure to stay that way (as in martial arts tournaments) then taking the fight to the ground and keeping it there may be to your advantage. Finishing the opponent on the ground can take time, is exhausting and is unlikely to remain one on one for any length of time in a real situation. In real fights your opponent may bite, gouge your eyes, seize the testicles etc. and this must be kept in mind during training.

If the fight has gone to the ground and getting up is not immediately possible, then you should scramble to find a dominant position. Holds do not just fall into place, they have to be fought for. When a hold is first secured, be prepared for the opponent to thrash about wildly as they try to escape. So long as the hold remains secure, this thrashing will be to your advantage as the opponent will tire rapidly due to the fact that a good hold takes nowhere near as much energy to defend as it does to escape from. As the opponent tries to escape, avoid pitting your strength against theirs as much as possible. If the opponent is moving to the left go with them, whilst keeping the hold secure, rather than resisting their movement. Should the opponent start to break free of a hold then go with the flow and quickly move onto another one. The important thing is to keep control of the opponent, not to maintain a single hold. Fighting in this way will help to prevent you from fatiguing as quickly as your opponent does and will help you to control opponents who are physically stronger than yourself.

To begin with, practice applying the holds on a compliant practice partner. When basic familiarity has been achieved, try to maintain each hold for 30 - 60 seconds whilst your partner tries to power their way out. This will pressure test the holds and ensure they are being applied correctly. Once you are confident that you can securely apply the holds, you should then wrestle with your partner whilst both of you attempt to gain and then maintain control. Be sure that this drill does not become a battle of strength and endeavour to flow from hold to hold where appropriate. Keep in mind that the holds are a means to an end and are not an end in themselves. Once you are confident with the holds it is vital you practice applying finishing techniques from all of them. The drills presented in chapter fourteen will allow you to practice securing holds and applying finishing techniques.

Hold 1 - The Mount

This position is undoubtedly the most powerful. From the mount it is possible to strike your opponent with force whereas they will be unable to get good leverage into their strikes. It is relatively easy to stand up from this position once the opponent has been sufficiently weakened. You can also finish the fight from the mount using a variety of locks, chokes and strangles. To assume the mount, place your knees on either side of your opponent's hips. Your hands should be based out above the opponent's shoulders, as this will make it harder for the

Fig. 1

opponent to roll you. Your chest should be firmly against the opponent's *(Fig 1)*. Should your arms become tied up, you can also stop the opponent from turning you over by kicking your legs out to the side *(Fig 2)*. Hooking your legs around your opponent's legs can help to maintain

Fig. 2

the mount if the opponent is being particularly aggressive *(Fig 3)*. As the opponent's struggling eases in intensity you can sit up and then begin to strike them *(Fig 4)*. If the opponent starts to turn, in an attempt to protect themselves from your strikes, be sure to give them the

Fig. 3

Fig. 4

room to roll underneath you in order to prevent yourself from being rolled over with the opponent *(Fig 5)*. If the opponent turns all the way over onto their front then you could raise their head by pulling the hair, or clawing the nose or eyes, and then apply a strangle hold to finish the fight *(Fig 6)*. However, regaining your feet from this position would be the preferred strategy unless the fight is guaranteed to remain one on one and you have no opportunity to escape (fighting in an isolated or secure area).

Fig. 5

Fig. 6

Hold 2 - The Scarf Hold

Place your arm behind the opponent's neck and, if possible, take hold of your own leg. Lifting the opponent's head off the floor will hinder both their breathing and movement. Use your other hand to grip your opponent's arm and pull it across your chest. Try to keep your head as low as possible and turn your face slightly away from the opponent in order to protect the eyes etc. from the opponent's free hand. Spreading the legs as shown will make it harder for the opponent to move you *(Fig 7)*. Should your opponent's arm become free, you can push the arm across, place your head tightly against their triceps and then re-secure the hold *(Fig 8)*.

Fig. 7

Fig. 8

Hold 3 - The Side Four Quarter

Lie across your opponent with your legs straight and wide apart. Keep your knees off the floor so that your weight is concentrated upon the opponent's chest. The arms are used to base out on the floor in front of you (Fig 9).

Fig. 9

Fig. 10

Bringing the knees in towards the opponent will afford better protection to your groin and give you more mobility, which will make it easier to stand up. The downside of bringing the knees in is the resulting loss of stability (Fig 10).

Hold 4 - The Upper Four Quarter

Your chest is placed onto the opponent's head. The legs are straight and spread out behind you. You should be on your toes in order to focus your body weight onto the opponent *(Fig 11)*. As an alternative grip - providing the opponent's clothing is strong enough - you can take your arm

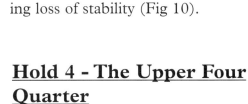

Fig. 11

underneath the opponent's arm and grip the collar of their clothing *(Fig 12)*. Instead of placing your elbows under the opponent's armpits, you may also pass

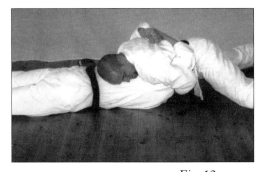

Fig. 12

Fig.13

your forearms under the opponent's upper arms *(Fig 13)*. This arm position makes the groin less vulnerable to attack but reduces the strength of your grip.

Hold 5 - The Guard

If you should find yourself underneath the opponent, wrapping your legs around their waist will help you to gain control. This position makes it harder

Fig 14

for the opponent to stand, prevents them from advancing into the mount, limits the use of their legs and also reduces the amount of finishing techniques that they have available to them. Interlock your ankles to secure the hold. The hands should grip the opponent's clothes, hair, neck, etc. so that the opponent can be pulled in close and hence prevented from getting leverage into their strikes. Once the

opponent is close enough you can pass one of your forearms across the back of the opponent's neck before clasping your hands together in order to secure the hold *(Fig 14)*. At an opportune moment you may open the guard and kick the opponent's kidneys using your heel.

Fig 15

Fig 16

Be sure to straighten the leg far enough before bringing the leg back, otherwise the kick will lack power *(Fig 15)*. The guard should open when you sense the opportunity to finish or escape. For example, you could finish using a choke *(Fig 16)* or you could escape using a knee lift *(Fig 17)*.

Fig. 17

Placing your feet onto your opponent's thighs is another way of controlling them from underneath *(Fig 18)*.

You have greater mobility from this position but your control over the opponent is reduced. Use your legs to prevent the opponent advancing into the mount.

Kicking one of the opponent's legs backwards whilst lifting the other leg will enable you to roll your opponent so that you can gain the mounted position.

Fig. 18

Hold 6 - The Hooks

Fig. 19

You will have a large advantage if you can get behind your opponent. Once you have got behind the opponent it is important that you do your utmost to stay there. Placing your legs onto the inside of your opponent's thighs and pushing outwards will limit the opponent's movement and hence secure your position *(Fig 19)*.

Should getting your legs hooked prove to be difficult, you can wrap your legs around the opponent as in the guard *(Fig 20)*. Holding on with your legs will make it difficult for the opponent to dislodge you.

Fig. 20

There are other holds, but a solid understanding of the six shown here should allow you to control the opponent from most positions. The key thing is to get plenty of practice so that you develop the ability to flow from one position to the next whilst maintaining dominance. I will stress again that the holds will not end fights in themselves. Holds are simply methods of securing a position of advantage to better facilitate the use of finishing techniques. Your aim when ground fighting is not to show off your skills but to end the fight as quickly as possible. Always be ready to finish the fight the instant it is possible to do so.

The most important thing to keep in mind is that should the opportunity to safely regain your feet present itself, you must take it without hesitation. If getting up is not immediately possible, you should use ground-fighting techniques to weaken the opponent until they are unable to prevent you from standing. Time spent upon the ground must be kept to an absolute minimum and totally avoided if at all possible.

CHAPTER 12

Fighting Dirty?

This chapter will look at the simple, effective and often unpleasant methods that can be used when grappling in high-risk situations. A real fight is nothing like a tournament match. Your opponent can bite, gouge your eyes, seize the testicles, spit, use weapons etc. There is a lot more at stake in a self-defence situation. Losing a real fight can result in permanent physical or mental damage, or even the loss of your life. Real fights are violent and thoroughly repugnant affairs and if you want to come out in one piece you have to be prepared to use violent and repugnant methods when it becomes necessary. All the methods in this chapter are recorded within the katas and in the classical texts but are now almost totally omitted from modern karate. As with many of the methods in this book, we should ensure that this element of karate is not lost if we wish to practice karate as the effective fighting system its founders intended it to be.

As martial artists, we should endeavour to develop high degrees of awareness and emotional control so that unnecessary fights can be avoided. We should always try to escape or defuse the situation before resorting to using our skills. If, however, the fight cannot be avoided, despite our best efforts, then we have a duty to ourselves to ensure that our assailant is not allowed to inflict their violence upon us. We have a moral and legal right to protect ourselves from unsolicited attack and to ensure that society's violent minority does not go unchallenged when attempting to damage our lives.

How you will fare in a real situation is largely down to your mental attitude. Your abilities to be aggressive and to cope with fear are important, as are your beliefs on the use of violence. Some people find themselves unable to inflict pain upon another human being and would rather (often by default) that it was they who were harmed. You must acknowledge that no one has the right to harm you. Your assailant is someone who gains pleasure or a feeling of personal power through the harming of others. You did not ask for the opponent to attack you. If anyone is to be harmed then it should be your assailant. They must not be permitted to cause you harm, and if preventing them from doing so means sticking your thumb into their eye or biting them, then so be it. Remember that when you cause harm to the opponent you will do so with a deep sense of regret that it has become necessary. When they harm you it is for pleasure or financial gain. In no way are you 'lowering yourself to their level' by using unpleasant techniques when it becomes absolutely necessary to ensure your safety. When you are defending yourself you can not allow any misguided sense of 'fair play' or of a 'clean fight' to place you at a disadvantage. In order to ensure your safety you have to be prepared to harm your assailant using whatever methods the situation deems necessary.

Methods such as gouging, biting and nerve manipulation require little skill or strength to apply and it is this that makes them so effective. A seven stone individual will have little chance of getting an arm bar to work against a sixteen stone assailant, however, with a well placed and hard bite they will be able to inflict considerable damage. When grappling remember to look for the obvious. In self-defence situations you must keep it simple, don't go chasing the fancy arm bar when simpler methods are available. Securing a grip on the opponent's testicles will win you the fight as surely as any choke, strangle or joint lock. It is the simple techniques that are most likely to succeed in stressful situations.

Before we go onto look at the methods themselves, please remember that they are only for use in extreme and life threatening situations. Be sure to use no more force than is justified.

Seizing the Testicles

The Bubishi contains a number of techniques that involve the grabbing of the testicles. An example of those techniques is reaching behind you and seizing the opponent's groin when being held in a bear hug. This technique is labelled as, "A guardian closing the door behind himself." The Bubishi also advises the grabbing of the opponent's throat and groin should the opponent secure a grip on the hair. The Bubishi refers to this groin attack as, "Holding something in place to keep it from moving." In his book, 'Karate-Do My Way of Life' Gichin Funakoshi relates a tale of how, at eighty years of age, he was attacked whilst journeying home one night. Funakoshi was courteous to his assailant and explained to him that he had nothing of value on his person. The assailant grabbed the umbrella Funakoshi was carrying and went to strike him with it. Funakoshi ducked under the umbrella and seized the man's testicles. The mugger let out a sharp cry and dropped the umbrella. At that moment a policeman appeared and Funakoshi released his attacker into the policeman's custody. As well as these examples from karate texts, the katas also contain examples of groin attacks. At the end of Pinan Godan (Heian Godan) the following movement can be found.

Fig. 1: Arms cross with the body weight over the front leg.

Fig. 2: Body weight moves backwards as the arms assume position shown

One of the applications of this movement is the deflection of a punch followed by an attack to the groin. The arm that goes behind the head to a 'soto-uke' position signifies that the pull should be made as strongly as possible in an upward direction. In the application photographs the trouser leg is seized as opposed to the testicles. The first part of the movement deflects a punch as a simultaneous groin strike is delivered. The groin is then seized, as is the opponent's jacket. The following arm movement will then push the opponent off balance as the testicles are pulled in the opposite direction.

*Fig. 3: Deflect the
opponent's punch*

*Fig. 4: Push the body whilst
pulling on the groin*

The groin can be grabbed from almost anywhere during grappling (vertical or on the ground) and is sure to take the desire to fight away from any male opponent. The testicles are very delicate and easily damaged. The groin should only be attacked when the severity of the situation justifies it.

Grabbing the hair

This book has already shown a number of hair grabbing techniques in the preceding chapters. Another example is found in Naihanchi (Tekki). The following sequence is found in the middle of the kata.

Fig. 5: 'Double Strike'

Fig. 6: Pull in

*Fig. 7:
Elbow Strike*

An interpretation for this set of moves is a hair pull followed by the elbow strike.

*Fig. 9: Move
sideways
pulling the
opponent off
balance by
their hair*

*Fig. 8:
Opponent's
arm has been
grabbed*

Pulling the hair will not finish the fight but (as in the kata example) can be used to unbalance the opponent and position them for follow up strikes.

*Fig. 10:
Pull the opponent back in &
deliver an elbow strike*

Eye Gouging

Attacking the eyes will have very serious consequences. A light pressure can be used to distract or disturb an assailant, but a harder pressure could easily result in permanent blindness and severe trauma. The eyes must only be attacked in extreme circumstances. The eyes can be poked with a single digit, clawed (as shown in chapter 3), or gouged using the thumb.

Biting

The Bubishi warns us about the danger of being bitten by an opponent in its sixteenth chapter which is entitled, 'Grappling and Escapes.' The Bubishi advises us to attack the opponent's throat the instant we are bitten and hence acknowledges the extreme danger that being bitten brings. The flip side of this is that should we bite our opponent, they will also be in extreme danger. The opponent is vulnerable to being bitten the instant any part of their body is near your mouth and a strong bite will go along way to securing your safety. How hard you should bite will be dependant on the severity of the situation. A bite that is little more than a nip can be used to distract or dissuade an assailant in order to facilitate escape, for example, a woman freeing herself from the unwanted embrace of a drunk. In extreme situations it may be necessary to bite a lot harder. The prime targets for bites are the ears, nose, lips and fingers, although a bite to anywhere on the body is likely to be effective. Biting is unpleasant, brutal and unhygienic, but it is also very effective.

'Fish-Hooking'

By placing a hooked finger inside your opponent's mouth and pulling, it is possible to cause great pain and to control the opponent's head. The danger of using the fish-hook is that it can leave the finger very vulnerable to being bitten. One way to avoid this is to place the tip of your finger at the corner of the opponent's mouth (Your left-hand to the left-hand side of their face such that you are reaching behind their head). You should then pull backwards and slightly out to produce a gap between the teeth and the cheek. Once the hooked finger is inside the mouth, keep pulling to ensure sufficient tension in the cheek. Master Chotoku Kyan defeated a Judo 6th Dan called Shinzou Ishida using this method. Kyan was visiting main land Japan in order to give a karate demonstration. Ishida had asked Kyan for a match in order to ascertain the value of karate. As Ishida reached out to seize Kyan, he moved to the side and thrust his thumb into Ishida's mouth. Kyan then stamped on Ishida's foot and pulled the off balance judoka to the floor by his cheek. Kyan then delivered a hammer fist to Ishida's jaw, stopping it just short of the target. Ishida was impressed by Master Kyan's skill and went onto receive daily instruction from him until he returned to Okinawa. The fish-hook can be effective when properly applied but should only be used as a last resort due to the high cost of failure.

Nose Attacks

The nose is a sensory organ and as such it is loaded with nerves. Manipulating the nose can be very effective. The nose can be attacked in a number of different ways. One method is to place your palm onto the base of the opponent's nose and then push upward as if trying to slide the nose off the face. This causes a lot of pain and will make the opponent's head tilt backward. If the opponent's head is secured against the floor this technique will be excruciatingly painful. You can also push the nose across the face using your palm in order to turn the opponent's head. The nose can also be compressed using the hand or forearm if it is prominent enough. The fingers can be inserted into the nostrils and then hooked, pulled or pushed (depending on the opponent's position is relation to yourself) to cause pain and to position the opponent's head for a follow up technique.

Grabbing the Ears

The ears can be grabbed and pulled in order to cause pain and to position the opponent's head. The ears may be used as an alternative to the hair for the various techniques shown in this book if the opponent should have no hair, or if the hair is too short to allow a secure grip to be attained. Grabbing both the ears as a means to smash the opponent's head against the floor is a common kata technique that is often misinterpreted as a downward double punch. Getting a good grip on the ears can sometimes prove difficult due to sweat etc.

Seizing the Throat

Grabbing the throat is a simple and effective technique that can be used to good effect in both vertical and horizontal grappling. Place your fingers around the opponent's windpipe and squeeze. This technique can be used to control the opponent whilst you strike them with your free hand. Seizing the throat is as effective as it is dangerous.

Finger Choke

Place your index and middle fingers at the base of the windpipe just above the sternum. Push both fingers inwards and slightly down. This method can be used to force the opponent to move away from you. The finger choke can be used to unbalance the opponent before throwing and can also be used effectively when ground fighting.

Nerve Manipulation

The Bubishi and Gichin Funakoshi's Karate-Do Kyohan contain diagrams and information on numerous pressure points that can be found on the human body. The katas also contain a great deal of information on the use of pressure points. A through examination of these points would be a book in itself. For our purposes we shall look at a few that can be rubbed or gouged whilst grappling.

Behind the ear (Dokko): Located just below the ear on the back of the jawbone. By pushing this point towards the top of the nose, the facial nerve will be pushed against the jawbone causing pain.

Under the Nose (Jinchu): Located just under the nose at juncture of the upper jawbones. Dig into this point with the large knuckles of the fingers and rub from side to side whilst maintaining the pressure to cause pain.

Inside of thigh (Yako): The insides of the thighs are sensitive areas that can be attacked by grabbing the flesh and nipping hard. Gouging at the top of the leg where the inside of the thigh meets the torso is particularly painful.

Under the armpit (Kyoei): Located on the side of the rib cage, just under the armpit between the muscles of the chest and back. Digging into this point, in the direction of the ribs, with a single knuckle and moving it up and down whilst maintaining the pressure will cause considerable pain to be felt by the opponent.

Lower ridge of the Jaw (Mikazuki): Located just inside the lower edge of the jaw, slightly forward of the jaw's angle. By pushing up and out at this point the hypoglossal nerve will be trapped against the inside edge of the jawbone causing pain.

There are many other pressure points but the ones described are both effective and easily accessible when grappling. Try locating these points, both on yourself and on a partner, to be sure you are aware of their exact location. If you are on the correct place the pain felt should be considerable. It is worth pointing out that the effect of these nerve manipulation techniques can drop considerably when the opponent is drunk or on drugs. The pain felt will also be reduced in a real situation due to the effects of adrenaline. This does not mean that nerve attacks are ineffective, it just means that you must be prepared for the fact that the opponent is unlikely to howl with pain and then submit the instant you apply them. Nerve manipulation techniques are to be used as part of an overall strategy; they are unlikely to win fights when used in isolation.

Violence is repulsive and brutal. Turning a blind eye to the more unpleasant aspects and methods does nothing to make violence less horrific, it will simply give those who perpetrate violent behaviour the advantage. If you wish to ensure your safety in a real situation then you have to be prepared to 'fight dirty' when the situation deems it necessary.

The key is to avoid the situation in the first place. Remember that the ultimate form of self-defence is a combination of awareness and self-control. A good martial artist should have both in abundance and hence violent situations can be avoided. When children get taught road safety at school, the emphasis is placed upon crossing the road without getting run over (avoidance), not on how to bounce off the car with the minimum of injury (self-defence). Martial arts should be viewed and taught in exactly the same way.

Putting It All Together

In this chapter we will look at how some of the grappling techniques contained within this book can be combined together and applied in a fighting context. As well as practising grappling techniques in isolation, you must be sure to make combinations a regular part of your training (in addition to the combinations that already exist within the katas). When fighting you must quickly take the initiative and then be sure to keep it until your safety is assured or you can escape. If your first technique does not stop the attacker then you should quickly move onto the second technique, then the third, and so on until the opponent is defeated. That said, be sure that you are not so concerned with the application of techniques that you miss the opportunity to escape. The instant the opponent is disorientated you should flee, if it is possible to do so. You should not go looking for a choke or an arm bar etc. when you could be escaping.

The number of possible combinations is infinite. Do not stick to the combinations shown in this chapter but experiment and create combinations of your own. Be sure that all combination techniques are effective and applicable. The key thing is to use the right method at the right time. Do not try to force a technique if the situation provides no opportunity for its successful application.

When you practice combination techniques be sure to keep all the movements crisp and precise. Try to get smooth transitions from one technique to the next so that the whole combination is performed in a flowing fashion.

As discussed in chapter two, grappling must be avoided at all costs. You must prevent the opponent from closing the distance and you must be prepared to deliver a pre-emptive strike should conflict be unavoidable. The technique shown below is in line with the methods prescribed by Gichin Funakoshi and gives one way in which grappling can be avoided. All the other techniques in this chapter assume that this first method has been applied but has proved to be unsuccessful.

Fig. 1

Initial technique

As the opponent approaches you, position one of your arms between yourself and the opponent. The arm should not touch or push the assailant as this is likely to inflame the situation. Your other hand should be positioned so that it is ready to strike.

The preparation to strike should be disguised so that it looks passive and does not warn the opponent that a strike is potentially imminent.

For example, do not clench the hand into a fist *(Fig 1)*.

Act in a passive manner and try to defuse the situation. If the opponent should become more aggressive and try to move forwards, the lead hand can be used to gently check their advance *(Fig 2)*.

Fig. 2

Should the opponent continue to move forward then strike the opponent, without warning, using the rear hand *(Fig 3)*. Whilst the opponent is stunned you should escape. When facing multiple opponents you should strike the one causing the greatest threat (normally the one closest to you) before escaping or rapidly striking the others. I strongly recommend you read **"3 Second Fighter - The Sniper Option" by Geoff Thompson** (published by Summersdale ISBN 1-873475-66-7) for some excellent advice on the ritual of attack and pre-emptive striking.

Fig. 3

Sequence 1

Fig. 4

Fig. 5

Head butt the opponent *(Fig 4)*. Quickly follow up with a knee strike to the groin *(Fig 5)*.

Place your foot between your opponent's legs and reap backwards as you push with the arms in order to throw the opponent *(Fig 6)*.

Once the opponent is on the floor deliver a stamp kick to finish.

Fig. 6

Sequence 2

The opponent has grabbed you with one hand. Deliver a rear hand uppercut to the opponent's chin *(Fig 7)*. Follow up with a reverse elbow strike to the base of the opponent's skull *(Fig 8)*. Pass your arm around the back of the opponent's neck.

Fig. 7

Fig. 8

Place your forearm across the opponent's windpipe and then clasp your hands together to secure a front choke *(Fig 9)*.

Fig. 9

Sequence 3

The opponent has you in their guard and has secured your head against their chest. Reach up and push on the bottom of the opponent's nose *(Fig 10)*.

Fig. 10

When the opponent releases their grip to remove your hand, quickly push their arm over the top of your head and begin to stand up *(Fig 11)*. Repeatedly strike the opponent in the groin in order to open their guard *(Fig 12)*. Stand up, being sure to keep hold of one of the opponent's legs *(Fig 13)*. Twist the opponent's ankle in order to turn the opponent face down. A groin kick finishes this sequence *(Fig 14)*.

Fig. 11

Fig. 12

Fig. 13

Fig. 14

Fig. 15   Fig. 16

Sequence 4

The opponent has seized your clothing and pulled you towards them. Put your fingers into the base of the opponent's windpipe and push *(Fig 15)*. As the opponent starts to move back, quickly place one of your legs behind the opponent's lead leg and reap backwards as you continue to apply pressure to the opponent's windpipe *(Fig 16)*. Once the opponent is on the floor deliver a stamp kick to finish.

Sequence 5

Both you and your opponent are kneeling. Pull your opponent forwards as you begin to move to the side *(Fig 17)*. Move behind your opponent being sure to keep your weight pressing down upon them.

Fig. 17

Apply a strangle hold as you pull the opponent backwards *(Fig 18)*. Fall onto your back and hook your legs into the inside of the opponent's thighs.

Fig. 18

Keep the strangle hold tight in order to defeat the opponent *(Fig 19)*. This technique should only be used if the fight is one on one and is sure to stay that way.

Fig. 19

Fig. 20

Fig. 21

Sequence 6

The opponent has pulled you over and is attempting to deliver a knee strike to your face. You have no option but to block the knee strike using the insides of both forearms *(Fig 20)*. Strike the opponent in the groin *(Fig 21)*.

Seize the back of the opponent's ankle and apply a leg lock to take the opponent to the floor *(Fig 22)*.

Fig. 22

Keep hold of the opponent's ankle as you stand up. Deliver a kick to the opponent's groin to complete the sequence *(Fig 23)*.

Fig. 23

Sequence 7

The opponent has got behind you and has secured both of your arms. Deliver a rear head butt to the opponent's face and seize their testicles *(Fig 24)*.

Fig. 24

Fig. 25

You may also stamp on the opponent's foot from this position or apply a finger lock to help break the grasp. If the opponent releases their grip take hold of their wrist and deliver a rear elbow strike to the opponent's ribs *(Fig 25)*. Take hold of the opponent's shoulder and execute a throw *(Fig 26)*. Once the opponent is on the floor deliver a stamp kick to finish.

Fig. 26

Fig. 27

Sequence 8

Your opponent is attempting to stand up whilst they are in your guard *(Fig 27)*. Keep hold of the opponent's arms as you open your guard and place your feet on their hips. Lift the opponent with your legs so that they are thrown over the top of you *(Fig 28)*. Let the momentum of the opponent's body start to roll you.

Fig. 28

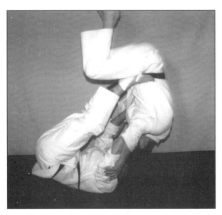

Fig. 29

Continue the roll so that you assume the mounted position. Use punches to weaken and distract the opponent before standing *(Fig 29)*.

Sequence 9

The opponent has hold of you and attempts to deliver a hook punch with their free arm. Move your head towards the opponent as you check the punch *(Fig 30)*. Deliver a palm heel strike to the opponent's groin *(Fig 31)*.

Fig. 30   Fig. 31

The strike will cause the opponent to lift their body weight. Move inwards and lift the opponent onto your shoulders *(Fig 32)*. Dip your head and drop the opponent onto the floor in front of you *(Fig 33)*. Once the opponent is on the floor deliver a stamp kick to finish.

Fig. 32   Fig. 33

CHAPTER 13

Sequence 10

The opponent has achieved the mounted position. Place your foot to the outside of the opponent's shin *(Fig 34)*. Wrap your arm around the opponent's arm, making sure your grip is secure *(Fig 35)*.

Fig. 34

Fig. 35

Bridge the opponent off you by lifting your hips and pushing to the side. The opponent will find it difficult to stop the roll due to both limbs on that side being trapped *(Fig 36)*. Quickly bring your legs over the top of the opponent's legs before they can close their guard *(Fig 37)*.

Fig. 36

Fig. 37

You are now in the mount. As you start to strike the opponent they may reach up and grab you in an attempt to pull you in close and hence prevent you from standing *(Fig 38)*. Grab the opponent's wrist and push on their nose in order to turn their head away from the extended arm. Step over the opponent's head *(Fig 39)*. Drop backwards to apply the arm bar *(Fig 40)*. After the arm has been disabled deliver an axe kick to the opponent's face before regaining your feet *(Fig 41)*.

Fig. 38   Fig. 39

Fig. 40   Fig. 41

Sequence 11

Grab the opponent's shoulders. Pull with one hand whilst pushing with the other in order to turn the opponent *(Fig 42)*. Move behind the opponent and begin to position yourself for a strangle hold *(Fig 43)*. Secure the hold as you deliver a kick to the back of the knee to unbalance the opponent. Keep the hold tight in order to render the opponent unconscious *(Fig 44)* - overleaf.

Fig. 43

Fig. 42

Fig. 44

Sequence 12

The opponent is attempting to secure you in the scarf hold. Place your forearm under the opponent's chin and take hold of your wrist *(Fig 45)*.

Fig. 45

Turn on your side as you simultaneously move your hips away from the opponent *(Fig 46)*. Scramble around as you push the opponent into the space you have created *(Fig 47)*. Push your forearm into your opponent's neck as you lift your head in order to break the opponent's grip *(Fig 48)*. Quickly stand and deliver a stamp kick to finish.

Fig. 46

Fig. 47

Fig. 48

The preceding sequences show how some of the grappling techniques can be used and combined in fighting situations. You are encouraged to create your own combinations and experiment with the various ways in which the techniques can be applied.

CHAPTER 14

Sparring

In a self-defence situation your opponent will do everything they can to prevent you from successfully applying your techniques. If you only ever practice against a compliant practice partner then your techniques will only work on opponents who actually wish to be defeated. To become a competent grappler you must practice your techniques in a realistic fashion. **Chojin Miyagi** (founder of Goju-Ryu) wrote in his **"Karate-do Gaisetsu"** (outline of karate-do), *"Through sparring practice one may identify the practical meaning of kata."* As well as improving technical skill, live practice will also help to desensitise you to the mental and physical sensations that are an inherent part of fighting. The pain, shock and disorientation that you may experience whilst grappling can be overwhelming. It is quite common for the mind to freeze due to the unfamiliarity and intensity of the situation. This inability to think whilst under stress will render all the skills you posses redundant and leave you at the mercy of your opponent. You must experience some degree of fear and discomfort during practice so that the brain becomes familiar with these sensations and hence will continue to function when under stress. This need for discomfort does not mean that training should be brutal, just that it must be made realistic if the students are to gain in skill and self-confidence. A good instructor will make the training character building not soul destroying. An instructor should never bully their students in an attempt to 'toughen them up.'

The fact that live practice is initially unpleasant leads many martial arts practitioners to either quit or omit it from their training. Worthwhile achievements do not come easy, nor should you expect them to. If you wish to be able to grapple in live situations then you must practice live grappling, no matter how unpleasant you may find it at first. The fact that you are prepared to practice in this way whilst others are not is a reason for self-congratulation, regardless of how well you actually perform. Be proud of yourself for taking the first steps and don't be too hard on yourself if you freeze or can't get anything to work at first. Stick with it and you will find that you will actually start to enjoy live practice and the techniques will get a little bit easier to apply every time you train.

In live practice your partner must fight with an aggressive attitude, if they come in close then you grapple, if the fight hits the ground then it continues and when striking, we must allow leg kicks, elbows, head butts etc. Safety is paramount during this type of practice. Remember that the aim is to improve your skills, not to inflict unnecessary pain upon your partner. To avoid unnecessary injuries ensure that there is proper supervision, suitable mats, pads and protective equipment. Control must also exercised on those techniques that can cause serious injury e.g. grabbing your partner's gi on the inside of the thigh instead of actually grabbing the testicles. Techniques such at biting and clawing the eyes should only be indicated during sparring. Lightly placing the fingers onto the eyebrows can be used to substitute eye gouges and gently nipping with the teeth will indicate to your partner that they are vulnerable to being bitten. Certain techniques such as strikes to the throat, violent neck wrenches and stabbing at the eyes should be omitted altogether. If a striking area is left unpadded then control must be exercised, for example, when head butting or striking with the bare elbows. Once your partner has you in a secure strangle hold there is little you can do to escape and even less benefit in fighting on. Tap out to signal submission, analyse what went wrong, and then start again. This type of sparring should always be closely supervised (one competent observer for each fighting pair). The observer must stop the fight the instant either party is in any danger.

If the fighters are injured (excluding things like cut lips, bloody noses etc.) then the match should stop. One of my training partners once seriously damaged his ribs by trying to fight on despite being in a lot of pain. There were three of us training and for this particular bout I was the observer. A take-down was executed during which my colleague suffered damage to the right side of his ribcage. Despite the pain, he insisted on continuing (ten out of ten for spirit - no marks for common sense!) All he could manage was an extra twenty seconds, during which he aggravated the injury so badly that he could not stand up and medical assistance had to be summoned. He suffered no permanent damage but was in pain for a number of weeks. If you are injured then tap out and call it a day. The match must stop if either party suffers an injury, whether they wish it to or not.

The actual boundaries and time limit for each match should be mutually agreed beforehand. If it is your ground fighting you wish to improve then start the fight with both people on the ground. If you wish to improve your skill at applying arm bars then agree that they are the only finishing techniques that may be used to win the fight. The possible variations are endless. What follows are a few suggestions on how you can organise your sparring bouts in order to enhance your grappling skills.

Type 1

An area is marked out on the floor. Both fighters take hold of one another and on the observer's signal begin to fight. No strikes, throws, holds, locks etc. are allowed. The aim is to simply control your partner so that they can be manoeuvred out of the area. The first person to leave the area is the loser. This type of sparring will improve your grips, your ability to control an opponent, your footwork, balance and will also get you used to being grabbed.

Type 2

The aim of this sparring drill is to take your partner off their feet. Both fighters take hold of one another and on the observer's signal begin to fight. All sweeps, throws and take-downs may be used. No striking, locking or ground fighting is allowed. If one of the fighters hits the floor whilst the other remains standing then the one who is vertical is declared the winner. If both parties should go to the ground then the fight stops, they regain their feet, and the fight is restarted. This type of sparring will improve your ability to use and defend against throws. Your skill at taking your opponent down to the floor with you, should you become unbalanced, will also benefit from this type of sparring.

Type 3

One fighter can do nothing but strike. The other fighter's job is to keep control of their partner's limbs and hence prevent themselves from being struck. The amount of control used is dependent upon the skill of the fighters, their physical condition and the type of protective equipment being used. This drill can be done vertically or on the floor. Regular practice will help improve your striking skills and your ability to defend against the strikes of your opponent.

Type 4

The match begins with both fighters on their knees, facing one another. On the observer's signal the fight begins. The fighters are not allowed to stand up, strike or apply any locks, chokes etc. The aim is to gain and secure the various holds outlined in chapter eleven in order to control the opponent. Remember to avoid using force against force and to flow from hold to hold where this is appropriate. This drill will improve your ability to scramble for holds, your skill in applying them and your skill at escaping from them.

Type 5

The fight begins on the floor as before. This time one of the fighters has to try to regain their feet whilst the other tries to keep them on the floor. Remember that in a real situation you must always try to get back to your feet once the fight hits the ground. This drill will help develop the skills needed. Preventing your opponent from standing whilst you remain on the floor is also critical in self-defence situations. Your skills in this area will be enhanced through the practice of this drill.

Type 6

Starting on the floor your aim is to get your partner to submit using locks, chokes and strangles. No striking is allowed and both fighters must remain on the ground. The observer must keep a strict eye on the fight and stop it the instant there is the risk of serious injury. If a submission technique is applied then the recipient should tap, upon which the technique must be instantly released.

Type 7

Both fighters begin the match standing up and a few feet apart. The aim is to throw your partner whilst you remain standing or to get a submission (either on the floor or when vertical). If the fight should go to the ground then it continues. Once on the floor the match can be won by standing up, when your opponent is still on the floor, or by the successful application of a lock or choke etc. No striking is allowed. Should both fighters regain their feet at the same time then the fight continues.

Type 8

Both fighters start on the floor. The rules are the same as in type six although this time strikes are allowed. If the blows are to be controlled, then you

should tap, or the observer should stop the fight, the instant that the blows would have rendered you unable to continue in an all out situation. The exact type and amount of blows should be agreed by both fighters at the start of the match, e.g. three or more head punches within an approximate three-second time period will end the fight.

Type 9

This drill is useful when either fighter has a specific weak area they wish to work on. Either one or both of the fighters is given a limitation on the methods they can use. For example, one may only punch whilst the other may only grapple, one may only kick whilst the other is free to do what they choose, one can only finish with chokes and the other can only finish with leg locks etc. The variations are endless.

Type 10

This type is the most advanced and should only be attempted by those with enough skill to ensure that the match is as safe as possible. The match begins with both fighters standing. Throws, strikes, ground fighting and submissions are all allowed. The fight ends when one fighter submits or when the observer stops it. If one fighter should be prone then the fighter who is vertical may deliver a single controlled stamping kick to the opponent's body to win the match. No hard stamps should be delivered whilst training due to the inherent dangers of such methods. As before, if the blows are to be controlled then the fighters should agree beforehand which ones will be classified as stopping blows. If the fighters have sufficient skill and appropriate protective equipment then the blows can be delivered with more force. Obviously no blows should be aimed at the groin, throat etc. The fight can be ended through submission or the observer's interjection for the safety of the fighters.

Not only will all of the types of sparring outlined above improve your skill in application but they will also enhance your fighting spirit, confidence and physical fitness. This type of training also becomes quite enjoyable once you become used to it. Live practice also gives you the opportunity to overcome fear, lack of confidence and other mental weaknesses. The overcoming of these weaknesses is a very empowering experience regardless of whether you actually won or lost the match.

Whilst sparring is undoubtedly very important, so are the katas. **Gichin Funakoshi** (Karate-Do Kyohan) wrote, *"sparring does not exist apart from the kata but for the practice of the kata"*. When practising kata you concentrate on yourself (understanding the principles upon which the katas rest). When practising sparring you concentrate on your opponent (applying the principles upon which the katas rest). Practice both and you will develop yourself both internally and externally and hence improve your fighting skill. Kata and sparring are not two different things; they are the same thing viewed from different directions and as such are mutually beneficial.

From left to right: Robert Gate 2nd Dan
The author - Iain Abernethy 4th Dan

CHAPTER 15

Conclusion

Defending yourself requires knowledge of kicking, punching and grappling techniques. The masters who formulated our art fully understood this and that is why a great many grappling methods are included in the katas alongside the striking techniques. This book illustrates a few of karate's grappling methods but there are many more. Kata is not a dead archaic ritual but a collection of highly effective techniques that were designed and perfected by some of history's greatest fighters. In kata practice we walk in the footsteps of these great warriors and have the opportunity to learn from them.

Adequate analysis of the katas will allow you to extract the techniques they contain. You must then practice the techniques with a partner. Once an understanding of the techniques is reached, you should take the principles upon which the techniques rest, and practice their use in other situations. It is also important to practice the techniques in sparring in order to get used to live grappling and to enhance your skill in application. If you approach the katas in this way then you can become a competent grappler.

The techniques within the katas were designed for use in self-defence against untrained attackers. Kata techniques were not designed for use against other martial artists in rule bound situations. If your aim is to compete in sport grappling, or to possess the skills needed to out wrestle a trained grappler, then it would be prudent to consider taking up the study of a dedicated grappling art such as wrestling, judo or jujitsu.

In real situations grappling should always be thought of as a last resort and should never be taken as the preferred option. In karate we only grapple when we have no other choice and, as such, the striking techniques have priority in practice. The danger is that too great an emphasis is placed upon the striking techniques and as a result grappling becomes totally omitted from training.

In a real fight the possession of strong striking techniques can eliminate the need to grapple all together. In both karate and self-defence, grappling should be viewed as a back up system to be used in the event of failed strikes.

Karate is an effective and multifaceted martial art. It takes decades to gain even the most basic of understandings. There is a vast amount of martial knowledge contained within the karate system. As I see it, the key to gaining this knowledge is simply to be honest with yourself with regards to your strengths and weaknesses, to practice on a regular basis and to be sure to train hard. Those who put in the work are guaranteed to reap the benefits. There are no short cuts. The level of competence achieved is proportional to how hard you are prepared to work.

BIBLIOGRAPHY/FURTHER READING

Karate-Do Kyohan by *Gichin Funakoshi* - Kodansha 1973

Karate-Do Nyumon by *Gichin Funakoshi* - Kodansha 1988

Karate-Do: My Way of Life by *Gichin Funakoshi* - Kodansha 1975

Wado-Ryu Karate by *Hironori Otsuka* - Masters Publications 1997

A Book of Five Rings by *Myamoto Musashi* (translated by *Victor Harris*) - Allison and Busby Ltd 1974 - Flamingo 1984

The Martial Artist's Book of Five Rings (translated by *Steve Kaufman*) - Charles E. Tuttle Company 1994

The Art of War by *Sun Tzu* (translated by *General Tao Hanzhang* - (Foreword by *Norman Stone*) - Wordsworth Editions Ltd 1993

The Art of War by *Sun Tzu* (translated by *J.H. Huang*) - Quill 1993

Ancient Okinawan Martial Arts 2: Koryu Uchinadi by *Patrick McCarthy* - Tuttle Publishing 1999

Classical Kata of Okinawan Karate by *Patrick McCarthy* - Ohara Publications 1987

Okinawan Karate by *Mark Bishop* - A & C Black 1989

Three Second Fighter by *Geoff Thompson* - Summersdale 1997

Animal Day by *Geoff Thompson* - Summersdale 1995

Real Grappling by *Geoff Thompson* - Summersdale 1994

Real Punching by *Geoff Thompson* - Summersdale 1994

Streetwise by *Peter Consterdine* - Protection Publications 1997

Floor Fighting by *Marc MacYoung* - Paladin Press 1993

Championship Street Fighting by *Ned Beaumont* - Paladin Press 1997

A Bouncer's Guide to Barroom Brawling by *Peyton Quinn* - Paladin Press 1990

Practical Chin-Na by Zhao Da Yuan (translated by *Tim Cartmell*) - High View Publications 1993

The Bubishi (translated by *Patrick McCarthy*) - Charles E. Tuttle Co. 1995

The Bubishi (translated by *Patrick McCarthy*) - International Ryukyu Karate Research Society 1994

The Bubishi: Martial Art Spirit (translated and edited by *George W. Alexander* and *Ken Penland*) - Yamazato Publications 1993

The Heart of Karate-do by *Shigeru Egami* - Kodansha 1976

Tales of Okinawan's great masters by Shoshin Nagamine (translated by *Patrick McCarthy*) - Tuttle Publishing 2000

NOTES:

NOTES:

NOTES:

PAVEMENT ARENA Vol 1.

The myth of Traditional Martial Arts working in the street is exposed once and for all. This dynamic video, which teaches many workable street techniques, is the first in a series of instructional videos by two of the country's leading exponents of Self Defence.

Peter Consterdine 7th Dan Karate, International Bodyguard & Author

Geoff Thompson 6th Dan Karate - Bestselling author and self defence expert.

£26.49 inc. UK postage and packing

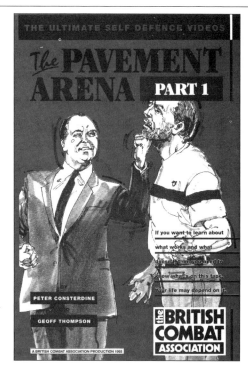

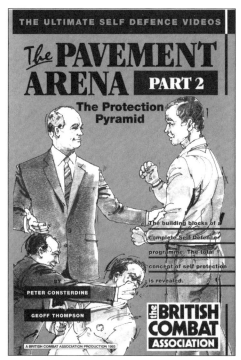

PAVEMENT ARENA Vol 2.
The Protection Pyramid

The protection pyramid provides a complete solution to the complexities of self protection. Each section of the pyramid explains a separate concept and is graphically illustrated with simulated violent street scenes.

£26.49
inc. UK postage & packing

To order any of these products or for our comprehensive product brochure - call our 24 hr hotline on
Tel: 0113 2429686

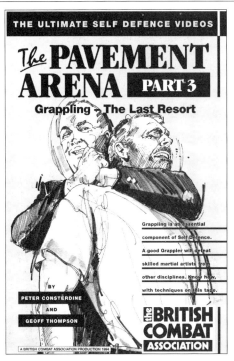

PAVEMENT ARENA Vol 3.
Grappling - The Last Resort

Once you have become involved in grappling with an opponent, you are there for eternity. There is no going back to a distance at which you feel more comfortable. You must know how to grapple and how to defeat those people who may be more skilled in other areas. Grappling will win fights, but there are a great many dangers involved - **Know How To Grapple - Watch This Tape!**

£26.49 inc. UK postage and packing

PAVEMENT ARENA Vol 4.
Fit To Fight

You need to be fit and strong to win a fight, but more importantly you have to develop the 'Will To Win' - the aggression never to give up and never to lose.
This mental edge is developed through hard training drills. It does not just happen. This video shows you how to train for strength, stamina, aggression and that mental edge.

£26.49 inc. UK postage and packing

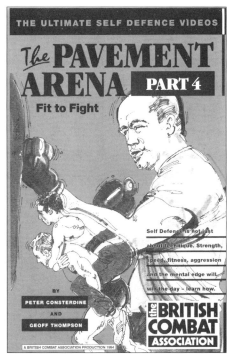

To order any of these products or for our comprehensive product brochure - call our 24 hr hotline on

Tel: 0113 2429686

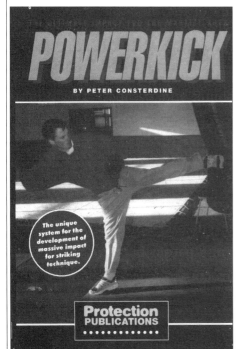

To order your copy of 'WATCH MY BACK' or for a FREE colour
brochure of Geoff Thompson's other books and videos call our
24hr hotline on:- 024 76 431100
or visit our website on:
www.geoffthompson.com